MAGIC FOR THE AQUARIAN AGE

A basic primer of magical techniques adapted to the needs and outlooks of the Aquarian Age.

By the same author:

EXPERIMENTS IN AQUARIAN MAGIC

MAGIC FOR THE AQUARIAN AGE

A Contemporary Textbook of Practical Magical Techniques

by

MARIAN GREEN

THE AQUARIAN PRESS
Wellingborough, Northamptonshire

First published 1983
Fourth Impression 1985

British Library Cataloguing in Publication Data

Green, Marian
  Magic for the Aquarian age.
  1. Magic — Handbooks, manuals, etc.
  I. Title
  133.4'3   BF1611

  ISBN 0-85030-318-4

The Aquarian Press is part of the Thorsons Publishing Group

Printed and bound in Great Britain

CONTENTS

This book is dedicated to William, Dora and Richard with love and gratitude. Bless you all.

INTRODUCTION

This is a book of wonders. It is full of adventures, of strange and unimaginable experiences — not those of other people, but ones that you can try for yourself. It unwraps the secret magical inner YOU that is capable of solving all your own problems, and assisting many of the people in the world around you. The only limits as to what you can achieve are set by your own feelings, and there are keys here to open the doors to a magical new universe once you have learned to use them.

Some books contain rituals and spells and expect the novice to feel safe and work competently through strange invocations, calling upon archaic gods and using words of power in languages few people understand. This book is not like that. It is a map exactly adapted for you, the seeker living at the end of the twentieth century, rather than the crumbling remains of an ancient rite which might have had some relevance in the fourteenth century.

Magic is a matter of experience and reality. It is a combination of inner skills everyone can develop, given time, dedication, practice, and the application of universal laws of nature. There are a number of magical exercises that have to be tried; there are the patterns upon which a personalized ritual can be built; there are notes on symbolism, divination and equipment to be studied and fitted into your own life pattern.

The Age of Pisces encouraged people to act like fish, all flowing with the tides and currents in a bunch, all doing the same things in the same way. Now we are on the brink of the Age of Aquarius when everyone will learn to become his or her own person, directing life and knowledge in an individual way. Each of us is different so each can apply these techniques, master the arts as an *individual*; and although the skills, methods and symbols are as old as the hills, they are still relevant if they are applied in the ways of the modern world. All the necessary keys are available to you in these pages. What use you make of them will depend on your commitment to magic, your patience and your determination to learn the old arts. No one can direct your path but yourself, guided by your inner self — and the gods and goddesses if you desire to know them.

To be effective all the time at magic requires patience and perseverance, but so does the acquisition of any physical or mental skill. Nothing can make you an 'instant magician', but if you follow the various exercises, ideas and experiments in this book, within a very short time you will begin to notice new perceptions, hunches and feelings of self-confidence.

This is not a book of old methods, ancient rituals and decayed ceremonies but an instruction manual, which, together with the parts and tools needed to build it up, can create for you a system that is not merely up to date, but is designed for your own future and for the twenty-first century, not the fifteenth. It may contain some surprises, some subjects that may not appear to be immediately relevant — but everything mentioned is important for the magical Aquarian Age. Consider each suggestion with an open mind, try the exercises, no matter how familiar or simple or unimportant they might seem to you now, and soon you will be able to judge the fruits of your own effort. You may well be in for some surprises, some new experiences, feeling; of health, of joy, and of being able to cope with the world instead of being swept along like a twig in a stream.

Read this book carefully: it may open your eyes to another universe. Have fun!

MARIAN GREEN

1.
WHAT IS WRONG
WITH THE WORLD?

Many people feel that there is something drastically wrong with the world and the way they have to live in it. Some people are content to suffer the miseries produced by this state of affairs, but more and more are becoming determined to *DO* something about the situation they find themselves in. This book is written for them.

Certainly, there is no simple answer, no miracle panacea that will instantly improve the whole scene, right the wrongs and grant a heart's desire — at least not in a manner one might expect. The world can be changed, improved and made the beautiful place of peace and plenty many of us dream of — potentially, it has all that is needed. What has to be changed is *us,* the perceivers of this world.

By changing our point of view, by developing our own inner skills, each of us can learn to help shape the world into the perfect planet everyone yearns for. I will not say this transformation is likely to be instant, nor is it easy; but anyone who has a vision of a better place, a happier state and a more peaceful and beautiful environment has the keys.

For thousands of years there have been schools of students taught in secret arts and crafts that have been called 'magic' because they were not fully understood. These ancient skills have been preserved and live on today. They involve methods of healing, of understanding the patterns and tides of nature and of working in harmony with these to gain the greatest help from nature herself. They help to explain man's position in the universe, and the part he has to play in its future. Most importantly, they have taught each individual to seek within and find the keys of his/her true self, and by understanding these inner strengths and weaknesses, become the best person they can. It is these particular skills that can be learned, and by altering the point of view from which we look at the world, we begin to see how distorted our former view of it was.

To get a clear view will require a lot of hard work, for in one sense you will be embarking on a voyage of discovery, climbing a new peak of personal experience, and that is no easy task. However, you will not be making this journey of exploration alone, for over the ages many thousands have trodden the hidden path, clearing the way and making the steps safer. Today there are thousands of people who realize that life has more to offer than may be obvious at first, and they too are travelling in the same direction.

This book consists of a number of exercises, both mental and physical, to help you to improve your body, making it fitter and more able to cope, and what might be called 'spiritual' or 'psychic' exercises. These are designed to awaken perceptions and senses that have been blunted by living in a modern, stressful world. Many of them may seem rather strange at first, if you have never tried consciously to alter your state of awareness, except for trying to fall asleep; but all are quite safe. You may think it odd that you are advised to try a different diet, or break old habits; but the objective of all these practices is to get YOU in total control of your SELF. Often it is easier to slop along, scarcely aware of what is going on around you, acting out of habit with no more will power than a caged animal. If you wish to improve your world, that will have to change — the comfort of following the herd, acting like an automaton, will have to go. You will have to take a grip of all your activities, physical, mental and spiritual, and you will soon discover what you have been missing all these years.

There is no reason why you cannot be extremely healthy, full of zest and energy when you wish, in control of your own life pattern and the way in which it unfolds, *if you want to.* Too many of us have forgotten what it is like to be really alive, although as children the summer days were golden and all was right with the world. To regain this youthful freedom you will have to be prepared to sacrifice some long-held ideas, to think in new ways, to act differently and to shoulder the burden of personal responsibility. You cannot go on passing the buck, or walking away from problems that you have caused with a clear conscience, if you become more aware — life just won't let you. The rewards for living life to the full cannot be estimated, but you will begin to feel liberated from a long term of imprisonment, during which you were your own jailer.

The secrets of ancient magic can be yours, but you will discover them only through experience. The exercises will need to be done, the experiments tried, the new experiences assimilated and thoroughly understood to get consistent results. Like learning anything else, magic requires practice and patience — it is not instant, although its results can be! Work steadily and you will be in for some surprises. Whatever may happen to you will be the result of some part of your self being awakened. It is in no way harmful, or 'evil'. It may seem strange, but then so is being able to swim, or balancing on a bicycle. Look upon it as an adventure that may lead you to explore new areas, discover exciting new talents, experience interesting and rewarding sensations, and get more fun out of life.

Identity
Today, many people are suffering what is called 'an identity crisis'. They are uncertain where they fit into the

changing patterns they see around them. Things used to be simple, organized and obvious; there was a clearly defined path from birth, through school, marriage and work to old age. Everything was straightforward; the roles and expectations were clear; the choices limited. Now things are changing at an ever increasing pace. Family life has altered from its traditional form of mother at home, father out at work all day, children (usually several) with their mother until the age of four or so and then sent off to school. Now children may only have one parent; they may be sent out to be looked after while their parent works all day; they may start school sooner, or even be taught at home.

This is only one minor way in which traditional patterns are breaking up, and the sudden shifts have caused a lot of people to feel insecure, afraid and puzzled. They cannot see where they fit in. They are not clear which goals they should be seeking. This unsettled feeling may in turn lead to depression, phobias, and all sorts of psychosomatic health problems. Some folk cling desperately to the old situations which, when forces beyond their control break up the old, seemingly secure base, are cast into a turmoil of new experiences and situations and are beaten down by circumstances. They may turn to drugs, alcohol or suicide, have 'nervous breakdowns' or other forms of mental disorder, not because they are actually ill, but because they cannot cope.

What this book is designed to do is to show people what aspects of their lives are under their own control; what skills they may be able to develop, given the right kind of instruction; what methods may be used to bring out all the most adaptable aspects of a person's character to help him or her through the changes. Many of these methods are very old and for a long time have been passed on by a teacher to one or a few pupils. Now some of these old techniques can be taught much more widely. They will probably never be universal, for what is clear about the people of today is that many of them are seeking individual paths through life.

How to Approach this Book

Certainly it is harder to learn by reading a book than by following the exercises or instructions of a personal teacher, but it can be done. The qualities you will most need are those of common sense and to some extent, patience. Like learning a new language, or taking on a different activity or sport, you have to learn the rules first, get used to the equipment, and try out different parts of the process until they are familiar. The same applies to these magical exercises. If you can follow the different sections carefully, mastering each skill before going on to the next, you will find that your 'spiritual' or 'psychic' muscles develop steadily and without any trouble. If you wish to rush ahead and try things at the end of the book first you may find yourself in the position of a boastful weight-lifter who is expected to lift a world record weight at first go! There is no advantage in rushing. The first skills are just as important (and may be the most beneficial to you as an individual) as some of the later ones.

This work is intended to be interesting, fun and satisfying. It can be learned alone or with a companion, or in a group. You can practice indoors privately, in the garden, in a park, or even, if the mood so takes you, at an ancient sacred site, stone circle or mound. You will need a minimum of equipment, and things you make or adapt yourself will give you greater pleasure than something simply bought for the purpose. If you have not encountered magic before, you may find some of the ideas and suggestions strange; if you are a practitioner already, you may find some of the exercises familiar. But whatever level you are at, you are in for some new experiences, which I hope you will find personally rewarding and permanently valuable.

Four cards from The Hermetic Tarot by Godfrey Dawson.

2.
QUESTIONS

'Who am I? Where am I going? What is it all for?' If these questions have been running through your head lately, you have begun the ultimate quest, which in one form is to answer questions such as these, and in another is perhaps the attainment of the Holy Grail.

In many countries people ask these questions and instead of turning within, where the ultimate answers must surely lie, they turn to 'experts', 'psychoanalysts' and 'psychologists' in the hope that other people can explain what they, the individuals, are about. Usually these experts will ask many questions and urge the wanderer in search of himself to make his own choices (which he will have to do anyway); but in doing so they will somehow make him feel more lost, more dependent on the good will of another and less sure of himself. There are probably a few people who do desperately need guidance to find themselves and to help them solve their own problems, but these are in the minority. Most people, given a fair share of personal honesty, uncritical self-examination and consideration, can go a long way in discovering their own motivations and needs. After all, only you can sense the mood of the moment, the inner need, the outward intention to express a feeling or fear. You can judge when you are hungry, determined or sad, and it is often an inner feeling that builds up to joy, happiness and contentment. By noting what things help to bring about these changes of mood you can gradually map your likely reactions to any situation. In time you can find ways to change a gloomy feeling into a brighter outlook.

It might seem daunting to have to look at and map your own feelings, but you can spend a few minutes each day thinking about how you feel. You can start by going through your life, from when you were a child, and jotting down in your own secret book the things you wished for, what you wanted to do, how you got on with the people around you. There is no need for this to be in chrono-logical order. Write notes as you recall them. You may also wish to enter today's ambitions and last night's dream.

From your own secret journal you will begin to discover patterns of your own emerging. This is the beginning of the magical journey of inner exploration. You are map-ping an uncharted country which you alone can visit totally. You can become your own expert and gradually, when you have lerned to change your awareness from the immediate world to the inner one, you will be able to make long expeditions to gain new knowledge. Be absol-utely honest in all that you write down. There is no need to explain or justify your feelings to yourself.

Self-knowledge
You might ask 'How is this a magical way?', because it seems so tied up with ordinary things. Remember that written above the doors of the temple schools of mystery teachings was the phrase 'Know Thyself'. This was the purpose of much of the old mystery teaching — to train the novices to come to terms with themselves as individ-uals, learning what practical and magical skills they possessed, and how, like any talent, these could be improved.

The reason for concentrating on understanding your-self first of all is because *you* form the core and base upon which your magical training is founded. The more secure this foundation is, the stronger and higher you can build. If you are aware of your own feelings or reactions to a given situation then you will be able to understand the feelings of others. You will become a crystal-clear mirror in which you may see other people reflected. By seeing yourself in your true colours you will be able to judge others, and knowing your own faults and failings, give them a fair hearing.

The simplest way to go about gaining self-knowledge is to get a small book, one that will fit into a pocket or handbag so that you can carry it about all the time. Start with your earliest memories; begin to recall your likes and dislikes. You can have a separate page for each and enter foods, music, situations, relationships — as many categories of items as you can. As it is secret, no one will pull your leg if you enter 'Dislike turnips' or 'Like cuddly toys'.

Devote another pair of pages to things you have wanted to achieve, such as learning to swim, riding a bicycle or horse, passing examinations, making friends, and so on. See how many of these you have done, how many you have abandoned and how many are still un-obtained. (It is never too late — Grannies take up hang-gliding or parachute jumping, or sail singlehanded around the world!) Have you done more things than not? Have you learned/mastered things which are useful to other people, or are your activities and abilities directed towards pleasing only yourself? Are your ambitions crazy, or are they reasonable, at least to you? Have they changed over the years, or do you still secretly yearn to drive a steam train or dance the lead in *Swan Lake*? Has the change in job availability or type affected your original choice of career, or have you seen new occupations or interests arise out of developments in technology, science or other matters affecting your life?

Change

The last few decades have seen enormous, and continuing, changes in almost every area of our day to day lives. But as the rate of change has increased, so more and more people are turning towards alternative philosophies and life styles in the search for stability and security.

The self-sufficiency movement has led many people back to the land, to try their hand at small-scale farming, animal husbandry and rural skills. Gurus all over the world have tried to do something similar in the realms of the soul or spirit, teaching the ancient arts of yoga, T'ai Chi, macrobiotic cookery, zen, and others. Religion has changed to try to meet the new needs of people in the modern world, though in so doing has sometimes cut itself off from the roots, which has lessened its value and impact on the world. Many people seek alternatives and ask entry to covens or cults, follow teachers of many colours in the hope that the inner turmoils that affect them can be cured from without. Many are sadly disappointed and come away disillusioned.

Although many teachers have valid messages, no one solution can possibly help everyone. The most important aspects of the human character have led to our survival in hostile environments – from deserts and ice caps to jungles and outer space. Human beings can adapt to new conditions, and this is why knowing to what extent each of us has been able to change and accommodate new circumstances is so important before launcing into the study of magical arts.

Magic was defined by Aleister Crowley as 'the art of causing changes in conformity with the will of the magician'. Similarly, Dion Fortune called magic 'the art of causing changes in consciousness in conformity with will'. In China, the great ancient oracle, still widely consulted, is called the I Ching, which means the Book of Changes. Change is magic, and magic is the art of making changes.

Once you begin to see how you were as a child, in what way you developed and what sort of a person you have become, you will be able to judge how subsequent changes have affected you. If you have been frightened and made uncertain by what seems to be happening around you, this basic understanding of yourself may give you a solid basis on which to build. You will learn to become calm; to cope with situations that once seemed beyond you; to flex and bend rather than stiffly resisting until you are forced into a different pattern. You will learn to *control* the changes, decide upon them and carry them out to suit your own purposes; but you will need to understand both yourself and the causes of change.

If you ask 'Where am I going?', the answer can depend a lot on where you *want* to go. If you have no clear plan for yourself, then you can so easily be carried along by every passing current. If there is a new religion, political party, or any other mass movement, and you have no definite plans, then you may be swept along with it, perhaps against your choice. You will need to list in your secret book the directions in which you would most like to travel on the road of life. In the fields of home, job, partnerships, friendships and achievement you may already realize where you would like to go. In each category it is best to look closely at the next step (preferably a small one) you need to take towards your personal goal. Gradually, as you progress through the arts in this book, you may find these directions changing too. Some goals will be fulfilled, but others will shift into a new and, at present, undreamed-of form. The surprises magic can bring into your life are totally unimaginable, until you step onto the hidden path that now lies at your feet. In a year's time, if you can look back at this moment recorded in your journal, you will know what this can be like!

Summary

It would be useful, perhaps, to sum up what has been said so far in this chapter. The purpose of magic is to help each individual become the most effective, competent and skilled person he or she is capable of being. No one can make you clever, strong or able to work helping or healing magic except yourself. Get *yourself* right and the picture of the world as you see it will change to a brighter, better image. You can change the world by cleaning the lenses of your self through which you view it. To help yourself you must obey the traditional command of magical schools throughout the ages — 'Know Thyself'. This can best be done by keeping a 'magical diary' or secret journal in which you record all your hopes, aspirations, ambitions and successes. You will need to note failures and difficulties too, for it is by balancing up the good and not so good aspects of life that you will find a pattern emerging upon which you can base future plans. You will need to be absolutely honest with yourself in this, for covering up faults will not show a true picture, and in any case your journal should be secret!

When you have considered the things you wish to achieve in the ordinary world you will be able to add to your list the things that can be assisted by magical workings. Perhaps you wish to act as a healer or counsellor to other people, or to be able to read the Tarot cards or the *I Ching* in order to see clearly what is to come. You might want to work on far-reaching projects such as world peace, justice or other global problems. All these things, and many more, are possible with a lifestyle in which magic is the name of a real art, as practical and effective as computer science.

The arts of magic are manifold and though most books tell you to 'believe in magic' it is better to learn to KNOW that these skills will produce results by personal experience. It is not a matter of believing that the light will come on if you turn the switch: you know it will. You may not understand how the electricity makes the filament of the light bulb come on, but you assume it will do so. Magic is the same. You may not be able to understand the stages by which what you will to come to pass actually does so, but once you have begun to get yourself balanced and tuned into the level on which magic works, you will know the equivalent action to turning on the light switch. The test of effectiveness of the various exercises in this book is simply for you to make a serious effort to try them. You can then convince yourself that magic is real, that it can widen the scope of your activities and add new dimensions to your life.

3.
MEDITATION: THE ART
OF STOPPING TIME

When Albert Einstein published his Theory of Relativity he put into words something which in ordinary life is a common experience. He explained that time is relative; that a traveller in outer space would experience the passing of time at a different rate to that of his twin brother left at home. This was a revelation in a world in which it was considered that time flowed sequentially, at a regular pace, measured in standard hours and minutes wherever in the universe you might be. Our actual experience of time, however, is much closer to Einstein's relative time, if you think about it.

You are bound to have been aware how time seems to fly past when you were enjoying yourself or absorbed in some task or entertainment. You will know too how minutes have dragged by like hours when you have been waiting for something to happen. Ten minutes at a bus stop in a thunderstorm can feel like an age, yet three hours watching a good film can pass like minutes. Our experience of time is personal and relative to our own scale.

Another aspect of our life in which time does not obey clock hours is whilst we are dreaming. During the periods of sleep which are called 'paradoxical' by modern researchers it is possible to see by movements of the sleeper's eyes, that he is following the action of some visible dream. This sort of sleep is called 'Rapid Eye Movement' (REM) sleep or paradoxical sleep, for though the sleeper might show brain wave patterns or electrical skin resistance readings close to his waking state, he would be very hard to awaken. In non-REM sleep his dreams are not necessarily pictorial but are 'thought dreams', and though measurements of depth would show he was more deeply asleep, he would be easier to wake up in this type of sleep. Whether they remember it or not, everyone dreams, and experimental subjects who have been awakened each time they begin to show signs of dreaming, and have thus been deprived of dream time, show symptoms of disturbance of memory and irritability.

Recent experiments have shown that there is another kind of dream, in which the sleeper is aware of being asleep and, without waking up, can communicate by eye movement that he has reached a stage called 'lucid dreaming'. Experimenters have conveyed information to the sleeper that has then been incorporated into the dream and recalled on awaking.

To meditate effectively is to reach an almost similar state. You will learn to alter the state of your consciousness, so that your immediate environment, worries, sensations, etc., do not concern you. You are totally aware and totally in control of the level at which you perceive things. This is a very old art and every culture has its own method of helping meditators shift the level of their attention. Some rely on techniques that distract the attention by the rhythmic chanting of a prayer, hymn or 'mantra', or by adopting specific kinds of physical posture, such as those used in yoga. These work because they occupy the attention of the mental or physical processes so that the inner levels of what might be called 'spirit' or inner self can begin to manifest themselves.

The Inner Self

Everyone has an inner self which may or may not make itself obvious. It is this factor that can take over in a crisis, so that people in accidents or dangerous situations suddenly find incredible strength or powers of endurance. It can also offer a quiet voice of guidance, helping with the very ordinary choices which life causes us to take all the time. We are sometimes 'urged' to act in a certain way, which we subsequently find out has got us out of danger, or brought about some fortuitous meeting. If you think about it, something of this sort may have happened to you. In the techniques of meditation outlined here, it is this inner voice, offering information, guidance or actual practical help, which proves so valuable in the everyday world. Your inner self has access to a great deal of information, part of which is derived from your own memories during every moment of your lifetime. It may also be able to recall material from your past lives. It is a source of wisdom available to everyone, and it is in this context that the following exercises are directed.

The thing most beginners in the art of meditation find hardest is learning to concentrate and relax at the same time. Many of them strive hard, clench their teeth, tense their muscles and try to force the meditative state upon themselves. It is like trying to make yourself fall asleep! What is required is almost the opposite — a state of mind in which you couldn't care less if anything happens, a relaxed body and an idling mind. It is surprisingly difficult to get into this state of 'turned-off-ness' without tensing up, worrying that nothing is happening, or thinking of some reason to give up trying and go shopping. It is easy in the beginning to be distracted by little itches or sudden thoughts because it is the inner self taking notice that you are trying to get in on the act. It is saying to itself 'Hey, who's digging in MY files. Who's walking through MY regions of this person? I don't like it and will stop it by making them twitch, or tingle or think about buying something. . .'. It is an excellent sign!

Because meditation is a way of stopping time, or at least your own awareness of it, it is necessary to find ways in which you can keep in touch with the normal world, once you get the knack. To begin with it is best to get rid of as many distractions as you can for instance, other people walking in just as you settle down, or the telephone ringing at a critical moment. Obviously, you cannot in all fairness order the rest of your family or household to be silent for an hour while you do your meditation; nor is it reasonable to hog the most comfortable chair in the warmest room at a time when others might expect to share that space. Be reasonable; choose a time of day when the house is quiet, when other people are not likely to use the room you have chosen, and when other distractions can be kept to a minimum. Do not make a song and dance about your new interest: quietly select the least difficult time and place with regard to those about you. As your expertise grows then you can talk more freely and perhaps share your methods with others.

One way of controlling the time of your meditations is to use a record of quiet, peaceful-sounding music as a background. This is useful in two ways: first, it covers up some of the noise which might distract you; secondly, it runs for a set amount of time, so that when it finishes it will help you to come back to the ordinary time scale as gently as possible. Select any tape or record which seems to you to be peaceful and calming. It doesn't have to be heavy classical if you like modern music, just as long as it has a lulling or stilling effect on you.

Basic Meditational Technique

Although many of the eastern methods of meditation suggest you should adopt a lotus position, squatting crosslegged on the floor is not a generally comfortable posture for most western people. Ideally, you should sit upright on a fairly hard chair with a high back. An old fashioned dining chair, sometimes known as a 'carver', with arms is very good. It will need to be the right height so that your feet rest comfortably on the floor (use a thick book or stool, if not), and support your back upright with your spine straight. If you need to sit on a cushion or place one in the small of your back to make it really comfortable, then do so. Later on you will be able to meditate sitting on a rock in a thunderstorm without being distracted by noise or discomfort, but it is best to make it as easy as possible to begin with.

If you have seen the pictures of the Egyptian pharaohs, sitting with their backs straight and their feet firmly on the ground with their hands resting along their thighs, you will know how you ought to sit for meditation, and pretty well any other sort of static magical work. Most people suffer from tension in the neck and shoulders and often this is a contributory factor in such things as migraine or other 'tension' headaches, upper backache or stiff 'frozen' shoulders. Usually these symptoms are caused less by the physical position than by a mental attitude of rigidity, which leads to stiffening of muscles and joints. If these sorts of things afflict you, the posture and practice of meditation may well help to get rid of some of them.

Some people like to meditate just before they go to sleep and feel that lying down in bed is a suitable posture; but too often, these folk get a good night's sleep but no advantages from their meditations. Others suggest lying on a hard floor, kneeling or slumping in a soft armchair; but in each case an extra strain is put on muscles, or discomfort or cramp forces the novice to give up the session before any useful shift of consciousness has taken place. Certainly when you have learned the technique you will be able to meditate on trains, sitting, standing or lying pretty well anywhere; but to begin with, do make it as easy as possible for yourself.

The upright position is best because there is less strain on your chest and lungs, allowing you to breathe easily. You will be in a balanced, poised posture, all your internal organs can rest in their proper places, and the nerves in your spine, particularly those in the neck, will not be compressed through being bent. For this reason it is important to learn to relax whilst keeping your head up. This ensures a clear airway and allows many muscles to relax. Breathing is used to help shift the level of consciousness at the start of a meditation, but you need to continue throughout the session. Your brain needs blood to ensure it is functioning as well as possible.

Once you have found a quiet time and place, perhaps prepared a tape or record of pleasing music, discovered a chair which meets as many of the criteria previously mentioned, and have asked not to be disturbed for a while — what next? You will need a notebook and pen, or a spare cassette or tape, so that you can immediately note any impressions, feelings, images and so on that come to you during the session.

Because the first part of magical training is concerned with learning who you are, a simple subject on which to begin meditation is your own ordinary name. Choose your first name as a setting-off point. On the matter of breathing, all of us breathe at slightly different rates, which can vary depending on what we are doing. You will notice that your own rate will vary during the meditation and other exercises. It is possible to follow a precisely timed sequence — for instance, 4 seconds breathing in and 4 seconds breathing out. However, this may be too fast for some people, too slow for others. If you need a natural rate to count at, use your own pulse, felt either with your fingers at the opposite wrist, or, if you concentrate, you may be able to feel it in your neck. You can even count heartbeats. Whichever you choose, begin by using a natural rate suited to your own body.

Sit upright, comfortable and still, with your hands relaxed and your neck balanced upright. Close your eyes and slowly say to yourself: 'My name is . . .' or 'I am called. . .', making each word fall on a pulse beat and breathing in for one set of words, and then out for the next. You may wish to hold your breath in and/or out for a couple of beats also. The pace is up to you. Just concentrate on getting a steady rhythm for the first few moments.

Allow your name to become the focus of your attention. You may hear people speaking your name, or see it written. You may sense others who share that name, or receive abstract impressions based on the meaning of the name. All sorts of things may flash through your awareness when you begin. DON'T try to hold on to these fleeting glimpses or you will find you have lost the thread. They will return stronger and clearer. When the music stops, or your time of about five to ten clock minutes elapses, stand up gently, stamp your foot firmly on the ground and jot down in writing or on tape immediate impressions, no matter how vague. If you think nothing has happened, say so. Meditation may not produce immediate results, especially for beginners; but as you progress, you will find that impressions, pictures, feelings and so on come both during the session and later, even in dreams.

You may well recall other items to add to your secret journal as a result even of the very first session working on your name. Jot down, too, how you felt — relaxed, cold, tense, wary, intrigued, and so on. Note any change in pulse rate, quicker or slower; any noises, feelings or other distractions which made it harder to concentrate, or even any fascinating revelations that your first session may have produced.

You might think these instructions are very basic, and that you have done this kind of thing before, but there are many people to whom this can be a new and rather strange experience and who do need to be gently guided until they get the knack of meditation. Even if you are skilled, you might not have tried all the experiments mentioned here, so give them a go, just for the sake of completion.

Relaxation
Some people find it rather difficult just to sit down and switch off thoughts and tensions that have been part of their ordinary life, so some simple exercises can often help to relax the body at least. So long as you have enough room to stand up and swing your arms a little you can do this in quite a confined space. The best results can be achieved by dancing to a record of your choice in order to loosen up your muscles and carry your thoughts away from worries or ordinary matters. Alternatively, try a few stretches and bends, especially movements which raise your shoulders, like reaching up. Twist and bend at

the waist, sway from side to side, always trying gently to go as far as you can with each movement. Very slow and controlled movements are better than fast swings, which could cause pain in joints or muscles if you are not used to this kind of exercise.

If dancing doesn't appeal to you, or if you have a health problem or are handicapped in some other way, you can still relax yourself before settling down to meditation. If you sit in your meditation chair you can clench and relax each set of muscles, starting with your feet. Ideally, you should remove your shoes and anything tight or uncomfortable. Screw up all the muscles you can feel in your feet, and then let them relax and become limp; do the same for those in your ankles, counting three as you hold each set tensed up. Go on to your lower legs and knees, then to your thighs, clenching them hard together for a count of three. Next the abdomen, solar plexus region, and the muscles of your chest as you hold a breath for 1,2,3 counts. Push your elbows hard against your sides and tighten the muscles in your shoulders, each time letting every part fall loosely to a relaxed pose. Clench your fists and all the muscles in your forearms, hold for 3, then let them fall limply onto your lap in a comfortable position. Next stretch your neck, raising your chin, then allow the muscles and tendons to relax. Screw up your face, shut your eyes tightly, clamp your lips hard together (don't clench your teeth or you might crack a tooth!); feel everything pull for a count of 3, then relax. Take three slow, deep breaths, breathing in gently as far as you can, and counting to see how high you can go, but without strain. Hold it for a moment, then breathe right out. This should be done without effort or strain. (If you smoke a lot or suffer from bronchitis, etc., you will not be able to take very deep breaths yet, but as you learn to relax things may improve.)

You should now feel quite calm, relaxed and at ease, and any problems which had been chasing round your head should have evaporated while you have been concentrating on getting your muscles to relax. Close your eyes and just 'feel' around your body for any areas that still feel tense and repeat the clenching and relaxing of any part until all is comfortable. Now, allow your name to drift into your mind. See if any images, feelings, or sounds sail by. Perhaps you will see what seems to be a film with a steady flow of scenes passing by, or still pictures, or just impressions – sounds or sensations that are vague and hard to grasp. Don't worry; allow your set time limit to run out, then get up, stretch and have a hot drink or a snack. Meditation is a 'knack'. For most people there is a period in which nothing seems to happen and then, quite suddenly pictures appear, or ideas begin to flow. Like learning to ride a bicycle, for a while you cannot get the hang of it, but then a little practice makes balancing easier. Meditation is the same: first you cannot do it, then you can, with no inbetween state.

Try to have a session each day, ideally at the same time, so that you are as awake and relaxed as you can be. Be patient and jot down ANYTHING that occurs to you during each session, even if it seems insignificant.

In the old schools of magic, the students had to meditate regularly three times every day. At sunrise they would begin by saluting the rising sun, whose light symbolized the spread of knowledge throughout the world. At noon, when the sun was at its zenith, they would briefly meditate on the work that they were performing and at sunset they would consider what they had achieved during the day. They would sum up their feelings, getting rid of any disappointments and failings so that nothing would trouble their sleep. This discipline was laid upon them from outside by the rules of the school. Some people still feel they need to be organized and made to do things at particular times; others are more flexible and are able to meditate effectively anywhere and at any time, though they should still perform a session at least once a day.

We are changing from the astrological age of Pisces, in which people acted like schools of fish, all following the same rules and the same patterns of life, to the new age of Aquarius. Aquarius is usually shown as a man with a water pot, pouring out a stream of water. This symbolizes individuality — people being their own masters and taking more personal interest in the way they plan their lives. The water pot symbolises those experiences gained by an individual that can be shared with others. Following the lessons in this book will help you become a better Aquarian person, self-sufficient yet able to share skills, abilities and activities with other people to your mutual benefit.

For this reason, rather than say you *MUST* meditate at dawn or at eight o'clock at night, it is best for you to find an ideal time to suit your pattern of daily activities, and which will not disrupt the activities of others in your home. Often early in the morning *IS* a good time, perhaps before the others get up and the house is quiet, or late in the evening when everyone else is occupied, watching television or in bed. Choose a time when you are not sleepy or concerned about something else. You may need up to an hour of peace in which to stretch and relax first, followed by meditation for ten or fifteen minutes and finally a period of further relaxation and recording your experiences.

You might find that exploring the concept of your name is unsettling and that you become lost in a maze of symbols and words. There is no reason to feel upset or contemplate giving up, for you are opening a channel to a part of your inner self that has long been overlooked. Obviously it may take a little time to free the line of communication. Everyone has good and bad experiences during their life: unhappinesses, actions you later came to regret, hasty words that upset someone close, can all leave a kind of scar or residue. This is sometimes referred to as the 'psychic dustbin'. It is a part of your personal memory where the 'bad vibes' or bruises left by the knocks life has dealt you seem to remain. Part of the training in magic is to have a dig around in this pot of past experiences and stop them getting worse and overflowing into ordinary consciousness. This is done, not by supressing them and trying to cram more bad feelings in, but by trying to look at each experience in the light of your current knowledge and see if it is really as bad as you thought at the time.

This is not a job to tackle all at once, but again by gently delving, a little at a time, you will find you can cope with things that seemed unbearable at the time. It is important to tackle these past memories because, for one thing, they will have taught you valuable lessons which you may not have realised, and the less junk there is in your 'psychic dustbin' the less chance there is of it causing you trouble later on. Quite often today's fears or phobias, dislikes or mental disturbances can be traced back to things that may have happened years ago and have lain bubbling away in your subconscious mind and now pop up to cause trouble. Although some people seek expert help from psychiatrists to delve in this material, it is often better to 'do-it-yourself', because you will not be embarrassed by thinking over former follies or heart-aches. Try it. You can either begin when you were a baby, thinking of the earliest events you can recall and coming slowly up to date, again jotting in your secret book, or start with yesterday and work back. Take a section at a time and honestly note everything which might be relevant. If you wish to be a successful magician it is important to understand what makes you tick!

One way for getting at the things you have 'forgotten' is to use a list of random words, meditating on each and seeing what comes to light. Open a book at random and point to a word with your eyes shut and then see what images and feelings it stirs up. Be patient. If you have lived for twenty or more years you will have thousands of experiences tucked away in your memory and you cannot hope to winkle them out in a few sessions. There is no hurry: the magical school term is as long as you need to master every stage. Only you can know when you have finished each exercise to your own satisfaction.

If you can share some of these lessons with friends or relatives you will find your companions may have different experiences to yours. There is no right or wrong way to experience things, nor is it bad to take longer to learn something new. Obviously, like playing a musical instrument, some people have a natural talent and will find it easier than others. The arts of magic are the same — some people learn to meditate, read Tarot cards, develop healing skills and work ritual much easier than others but in every case, patience and perseverance will pay off. You can never try for too long, though: because meditation requires a relaxed body and alert mind, it is possible to try too hard! The mind is a butterfly, not a log, and needs dealing with accordingly - although it can behave like a log sometimes!

Using your own name as a focus, allow images, feelings and impressions to come to you. Although you will be very relaxed and become able to sink deeply into the meditative state, you will still be aware of your surroundings, able to cope with any emergency or other matter if the need arises. Remember, you are in charge and can control the speed of the process and the material which you explore. You are starting with yourself, for only by understanding your own life and motives can you reasonably hope to begin to understand what makes others tick. By exploring and turning out the contents of your memory's 'psychic dustbin' you will be able to cope with some of your fears and past unhappinesses. Magic will lead to a fuller, happier and more beneficial life for you and those around you.

Practise regularly, noting all your discoveries, for when you come to look back you will be amazed what has come to light, even in blank periods; for dreams, ideas and sudden inspiration can all enlarge or clarify the picture, even if meditation does not seem successful initially. Be patient, for you are a novice in an art that is thousands of years old. No one can be expected to become an expert in a few days, but surprisingly, many people get the knack quite quickly and start to uncover a vast source of information and guidance.

Though to begin with even ten minutes may seem a long time to try to wring information out of your inner self, as your technique improves time will begin to flow by without any awareness on your part. Real experts can sit motionless in meditation for many hours; but avoid forcing long sessions on yourself until you feel you can cope. You should always feel completely alert, aware and 'back here' after a session. Should you feel sleepy or confused you will need to be firm with yourself: take some deep breaths, stamp your feet and move around vigorously. Often a hot drink or piece of fruit will get the system going. You may also feel cold if you are sitting still for a long time in a cool room, but you will soon recognize these things as ordinary happenings and you can wrap up, or sit more comfortably to get rid of any disturbances.

Often you will hear your heartbeat, the gurglings of your digestive tract, feel your pulse beating and be annoyed by itches, tingles or odd feelings. These are quite natural and most of the time they happen without your noticing. They are a good sign in that you have begun to turn your attention away from the outer world and are sensing the complicated inner world, perhaps for the first time. Your breathing will tend to slow down and so will your pulse; you ought to feel relaxed but full of energy once you get into the swing of meditation. Even things like tension headaches, neck strain and odd aches and pains can be alleviated by regular sessions. Once you have come to grips with the 'inner you', you can tackle your general health and try the suggestions later on designed to help you become a fitter and stronger person.

4.
VISUALIZATION: CREATING A PLACE IN INFINITY

Meditation is an altered state of consciousness in which you cease to be concerned with the time and place in which you are sitting and enter a world of information affecting various senses. It is an inward-looking, waiting and perceiving state in which impressions and feelings can make themselves felt. It is an essentially passive activity, for apart from continuing to maintain a relaxed and attentive state you are not directing the material that comes to you. Creative visualization, on the other hand, is a method of directing what you see and of creating, from fragments already in your memory, a new place or condition. It is the most important key to practical magical work and allows you to direct your will effectively, through the images you create. To do it effectively is not easy.

You will learn to direct your 'mind's eye' to any place or imaginary situation with accuracy and clear vision. To begin with, you should concentrate on things or places you can actually visit, so that you can check the images you perceive against the real thing and be certain you are not deluding yourself. Magic is an art of reality just as cookery. You cannot throw together any old picture and expect it to be true to life, just as you cannot throw together any combination of foodstuffs and expect a perfect fruitcake. There is a right way to do both.

To begin with, you will need to repeat the same sort of relaxation exercises that you did before meditating. If you do not receive useful information from that, there is little point in trying visualization just yet. Once you are still and relaxed, you should imagine that part of you can see through your closed eyelids. Try to picture or sense (not everyone gets actual pictures) some object in the room with you: a vase, a book, the cover of a magazine or the pattern on the curtains — it doesn't much matter what. See it in colour, sense its texture, focus on a detail — is it real, is it solid, does it stay there for you to examine? Usually not, to begin with. Objects become vague, colours and patterns shift, detail blurs. Open your eyes and look at it. How does the actual thing differ from your impression of it? Examine it, and then try again.

It is very important to be able to see an actual object clearly and in a real and lasting way, because during your magical work you will be presented with all sorts of images, symbols, illustrations, objects and pictures which you will need to remember in order to interpret them. It is no use saying to yourself, 'I think I saw a red triangle, or it could have been an orange dagger, or perhaps a thing like the top of an iron fence gone rusty. . .'. You will need to see, quickly and accurately, whatever may come your way, and it is no use pretending: you will have to learn at least to get clear impressions, every time.

The human eye can act with extreme definition and can detect thousands of variations of colour and texture, distance and depth. The brain then interprets the data the eye picks up, and from its store of memories identifies and names what is being seen. Even if you see something for the first time your eye and brain will tell you it is a flower, a machine, a soft, slimy substance. Think of the way children learn to name and recognize things. Within a few years of life, they know the names of colours, objects, foods and so on. Recent studies have shown that they can even recognize numbers of dots and do sums and subtractions before they are able to recognise the numbers written as figures.

Most people use about 8 per cent of their brain. If you try very hard you might get it up to 10 per cent. This unused capacity may be full of memories, or is just waiting to be exploited through the use of 'psychic' senses. You can improve your ordinary vision and concentration by taking notice of things about you. Look at shapes, colours and the natural world about you. Try to match designs of things seen as patterns on wallpaper with real flowers, etc. Imagine the colours of things and see if they are just as you imagined them. Ask yourself about the shapes of leaves, the way a tree branches — did you know they are all different? What about flowers, fruits, vegetables — what details do they share?

Shut your eyes and see a Rolls Royce car. What details come to mind? What about a wild rose? A tabby cat? A giraffe? Your memory is bound to be crammed with information on all sorts of animals, plants and objects, especially since most people have been exposed to films, television, illustrated books and so on for many years. Perhaps you have never touched a panda, but you know what it is like. When you learn to use visualization creatively you may be able to make one to play with, to feel and to talk to!

Inner Vision
Magic has always relied upon symbols and upon the use of items of equipment which may seem archaic or clumsy at the end of the twentieth century, but these are very powerful in the world of inner reality. In really elaborate rituals there are long lists of instruments, regalia, banners, altars, signs and symbols and to use all of them could mean a considerable outlay of cash. Many of these items can be seen in the mind's eye, or represented by some more ordinary objects, which, for the duration of the ceremony, appear to be the magical equivalent.

Just as a name can call to mind a whole series of

impressions, so any symbol traditionally associated with ritual magic will evoke, on some inner level, a great collection of similar associations. It is these associations that make it such an effective and powerful symbol, and why, after hundreds of years, it is still used by modern magicians. There certainly is a case for gathering at least some of the symbolic objects as your personal tools, so that you can get the feel of practical work. It is much easier to remember the feel of an act if you have actually done it. If you have wielded a sword, or received a cup in a communion, felt the weight and grip of a magical wand and carved the design on a platter, it is much easier to imagine these items.

Magic is a matter of experience. Some things you can effectively imagine, but if you have personal experience of them it will be much easier. The equipment can be purchased from specialist shops, or you can do the whole thing by pretending the stick in your grip is a sword; but if you can find the determination to gather the basic equipment, making some items, altering others, you will have the most powerful tools available to you. You will need to try all sorts of practical things as you gain the skills of modern magic, just as the novices learned in the old schools. You will have to learn from a book instead of a teacher, but you can increase your own abilities by actually trying things, as best you can.

Back to the subject of visualization. You should try to fit in a training session each time you meditate. Look at an object, close your eyes and try to 'see' it, in colour and three dimensions, then see if you can alter details. Can you change the colour, the size, the shape or texture? If you can, it is imagination not a true vision. The thing is real so it has a fixed form – try to learn that.

Another test of your ability to really 'see' is to imagine what is on top of things in your house. Look through closed cupboard doors, inside drawers, anywhere that you have not examined recently. Once you have a clear impression, go and look! Were you right?

The reason that clear inner vision is so important is that if you begin to work on seeing into the future you will need to recognize any details that may confirm your vision. If you see a date on a calendar, for example, you will want to know what it actually is, especially if you are being warned of danger to yourself, or someone close. Car numbers, details of places, clothing, the state of flowers or trees can all help to indicate the season, place and the people involved. The more observant you become in ordinary everyday matters, the better you will be at magical seeing. In both cases it can matter. Imagine you are the only witness to a crime and can recall clear, accurate details of what happened — you could prove a valuable witness and perhaps prevent a second crime.

Experiments with hypnotic subjects have shown that when relaxed in a hypnotic state considerable details of forgotten events can be called to mind. The same can be true of anyone who has deliberately altered his own state of consciousness in the relaxed pose of meditation, for by remaining in control he can carefully examine anything he sees. In both hypnosis and in meditation the state is actually controlled by the individual whose state of consciousness is being altered. No one can compel a change of state: it has to be voluntary. The more you are in control, the more information can be discovered. The data is there, it is the recall system which needs to be tuned up!

The Magical Personality
Visualise yourself as you imagine other people see you. Are you generally cheerful or gloomy, smiling or glum? Do you have many friends or none; lots of acquaintances, or are you always surrounded by familiar strangers? What do you think others feel about you? Do you feel lonely, alienated or are you constantly surrounded by loving friends and people you often hug and kiss? One of the other applications of creative visualization is used to create what is known as a 'magical personality'.

If you are disappointed with the way you are seen by others, or have become aware of parts of your character that could be improved in some way, now is your chance. Traditionally, the magical image a person creates is one of an adept, surrounded by novices and holding a position of power and domination within the magical lodge. In real life modern magic, this image is the magician who has become totally himself/herself. Each of us has many talents and skills that have been overlooked, and aspects of ourselves that have been repressed by the world in which we live. By acknowledging that we can all be more effective human beings, and by striving in various ways to improve ourselves, we can make our world a better place for us, and more important, make it a better place for those around us.

Some of the old rituals talk of the 'perfect self', the 'true person', the 'higher' or 'inner self'. We do have an 'inner self' and if this aspect can be encouraged to show itself and work through our lives we can grow to match the magical image of our personality. Perhaps you wish to change your shape, be thinner or more curvy, stronger or more appealing to other people. To a certain extent these changes can be made, for once you determine to alter the body it will help you to change the way you live. You can 'think' yourself fitter, quell minor and some major ills, become the magical image you see before you. All it takes is time and the will to make it happen.

Perfection is not a boring, self-righteous state in which you criticize everyone about you, but a widening of all your horizons. If you can see more of the picture you can see where different factors fit into it; you can detect patterns which the narrower, unclear view cut out. By raising your state of awareness you can sense the needs, abilities and troubles of others, and if you have gained knowledge, skill or understanding, you can help them. As you help others, you help yourself, for through their improvement the whole world is made a fraction better, even for you. You also gain experience. Probably you will not achieve 100 per cent perfection all at once, but think how much fun, interest and new experience you will gain in the process. Life is infinitely more strange, thrilling, and fascinating than you can possibly imagine, and the only things stopping you seeing it are the spectacles you have chosen to wear, or which circumstances have forced upon you. (It is not your physical vision, which may also need correction, but your inner view of reality that may be at fault!)

Through experiencing the images creative visualization can show you, and by learning to see things as they are, you are moving into a greater, virtually infinite world of visions. By recognising what you see as real now, you can create a new future for that scene in which things can be changed for the better. If you have a broken leg, for example, you can see yourself out of plaster, running and jumping with no pain and full strength; you can then work towards that result. See yourself getting stronger, the bones knitting straight and firmly, as quickly as possible. It can happen!

You may need something and by creating an image of it, draw it to you. You will begin to find information you require suddenly turning up, books even throw themselves off shelves and fall open at the relevant page on occasions! You will find your meditations show you the location of bargains, or where some out-of-the-way object you want may be found. Lost items may show their hiding places and turn up even after you have searched thoroughly.

By using meditation and visualization together you can uncover all sorts of valuable information. Visualize the thing or situation you require and then meditate upon it. A clear picture or strong indication may well come to you if you are patient. Often the solutions to difficult problems can be found, and those difficult inter-personal relationships be untangled by submitting them to the inner wisdom and clear sight of your meditative self. Don't be selfish, either. It does pay in magic to use your new found skills for the benefit of other people. Don't meddle, though. Many of the experiences life throws at us are for a purpose that may not be clear at the time, but later on will be seen to have taught us a valuable lesson. If other people are having troubles, help as a friend but do not expect to be able to wave a wand and make their difficulties vanish in a puff of smoke. It does not work like that. Give advice if you are asked for it, or support them through the tough time, in a way you would like to be supported in similar circumstances, but let them gain whatever experiences are there for themselves. Meditate to see what might happen, and if that produces helpful information pass it on, but do not make a song and dance about inner inspiration. Most people do not understand and you might lose a friend in consequence. Magic is meant to be a secret, so be discreet.

Try to have a session of meditation and visualization each day so that these two key techniques become second nature. Without them, the other arts of magic and of self-awareness are impossible.

Pathworking

If you have a friend to share your work with, or else a tape or cassette recorder, you can try another application of visualization and meditation which is used by most magical groups. This is usually called 'path working', named after an exercise concerning the Tree of Life, the central glyph used by students of the Qabalah, a Hebrew mystical system. What happens is that a journey is described by one person and everyone tries to 'see' the scenes or images as clearly as they can. Sometimes people take it in turn to continue the story, or take up the narrative as the mood takes them. Others add details or tell of their own impressions as the visualization is continued. This is a very natural way to encourage magical vision because it is one we have known since childhood. Almost everyone has had stories read to them and have imagined the characters, scenes and events as they were read. A vivid imagination, directed by magical training, is the most effective tool we have for changing the world, and it is something which has often lain dormant since childhood. The world of fairies is still there, but our adult eyes tend to look through it. We can regain the dimmed sight if we so wish, and with it see infinity, explore the far side of the moon, visit the lands of lost legend and the power that lies there.

Ideally, you should have a companion to read the words to you, pausing here and there to allow the pictures to grow real and solid. If you are alone it is possible to read the narrative onto a tape and listen to it as you are meditating. Go slowly until you remember the child's skill of sensing the details, seeing any characters who turn up, and feeling the atmosphere. If several of you share this experience, take it in turn to read. There is a skill in that, too, which can be learned with practice. It is also good training for reading and performing rituals with others, as it helps you get over stage fright or embarrass-ment. Allow yourself plenty of time for relaxing first, for going through the script, and for pausing where there is a place to receive new impressions or information. You may need a while to jot down ideas afterwards too, so do not try to fit in a rushed session between other appoint-ments. It can be fun and is a very good way of getting used to sharing magical experiences, so make sure your companions are not in a hurry either.

A simple example of the idea which you might like to try involves an imaginary journey to a place that is quiet, peaceful and calming, and where it is easy to sink into an altered state of awareness to commune with the 'inner you'. For this particular exercise, a beach scene has been chosen because it implies a holiday away from the everyday sights and tensions. If you prefer a woodland glade, a mountain path, the interior of a large and beautiful house or a wild and lonely moor, then, using the same sort of pace and imagery, invent your own path.

Get yourself into a meditative frame of mind, make sure you will not be disturbed for about half an hour. If you are not able to record the narrative, read it through a number of times until you can recall the various stages and tell it to yourself without having actually to read the text. You need to be as relaxed and comfortable as possible, and work steadily through the images at your own pace.

Imagine you are walking along a path among short pine trees and sweet scented shrubs. It is a warm sunny afternoon and there is a light breeze carrying the smell of the sea. You stroll slowly, basking in the warmth. Soon the path turns a corner and begins to slope gently downwards, zigzagging along the face of a golden, sandy cliff. Below is a long beach of pale sand, here and there dotted with rounded boulders of a darker reddish colour. At the foot of the cliff path you pause, touching the rock and finding it warm and soothing under your fingers. The tide is coming in and there is a narrow belt of weed and shells rippling along the beach. No one is in sight. Turning to the left you walk along the base of the cliffs, which rise and darken in colour to an almost russet red. You see where rain and tide have formed steep canyons or shallow caves in the soft sandstone. Along the top, like a green fringe, hang swathes of grasses and small weeds with white, red or yellow flowers. It is very quiet and the small waves make a soft, swooshing sound as they run in over the firm sand.

After walking a distance from the cliff path you notice a rounded boulder which is just right to sit on, and with your back against the sandy cliff, you sit, and look about you. In both directions the beach curves inwards to form a large bay. In the distance you can see small white houses clustering beneath red tiled roofs among deep green pines. It is very warm and you look out to sea. The water is clear and the small waves break translucent greeny-blue with white foam on the tawny shore. Although the sea is calm you can sense its power, which is shown by the deeply-etched cliffs and the worn-down rocks. You can imagine it pounding the beach in a storm and tossing great ships about in a smother of foam. You can feel the pull of the tides, and you recall that man is made up largely of water. There is a natural ebb and flow of things in your life, and sometimes it has seemed as if a great wave has swept away things you did not want to lose. The tide of seasons works on land as it does in the oceans, but the earth tides are slower. For a while you pause and consider all this. . . .

Looking up into the clear blue sky you see the sun and feel again its heat upon your skin. Here it is mild yet in a desert it can dry and wither all who stray beneath its rays. It has the power to bring forth life in spring, yet it can scorch and shrivel the life it calls forth. Without the sun's heat, this world would be a dead speck of ice in a sunless night. You think of heat as anger, power or energy and remenber the warmth of love, the fires of passion and perhaps having a hot temper. It brings to mind all sorts of memories. . . .

Lowering your glance from the hot sky you notice a small yacht, with white sails slanted against the wind. You feel the breeze on your cheek and scents of land and sea waft past you. Perhaps the smell of cooking awakens a memory of a past meal, or the scent of flowers a walk in a sunlit garden. Maybe there is a tang of seaweed or of flames quenched by rain from long ago. The wind may bring you the keys to many past experiences, for the scents can release long forgotten incidents and call them to mind. The oily shrubs may smell like incense; mown grass or the sea itself may awaken dreams of childhood holidays. The store of memory is opened and many images and feelings flood over you. For a long moment you are enthralled and absorbed in these. . . .

On the wind comes the cry of a gull, and the distant murmur of traffic. A boat engine roars out to sea, and above you on the cliff children's voices call and chatter. Their laughter reminds you of your youth and the other sounds compel you to take notice of the present. You know that you cannot sit dreaming for too long, and that there are tasks and duties that need to be performed. Gradually, you rise and return along the beach. The tide has come in and the sand is narrowed at the foot of the cliff. You cannot prevent the tides of the sea or the land returning and must move with them.

Soon the foot of the path is reached and you walk lightly up its twisted track. You feel refreshed and filled with sunlight and a clean wind. You breathe deeply and freely, and feel as if you have cast off a heavy burden. You have regained a little of the childlike freedom of spirit. Slowly you return to your own room, your own place, opening your eyes to today's world.

Do not rush to get up but stretch and yawn. Have a good shake and perhaps a drink or snack to get you back into the here and now. You may be surprised how much time has passed during your 'holiday at the seaside'. You should feel good, both relaxed and calm, and you will be filled with energy. If you do not feel right you may need to try this exercise a few times to get the hang of it. No magical exercise should make you feel weary or tired or otherwise unpleasant. They are mostly based on relaxed and aware states, and so it is only your mind that has been working. Any feelings of strangeness are due to the fact that you are re-opening old channels between your imagination and your conscious mind. Each half of your brain is concerned with a different sort of perception and these magical journeys are aimed at forging closer links and clearer channels along which information and perception may flow. If these paths of communication have become silted up it may take a bit of work to free them. Do not give up if you didn't get a great deal the first time.

At each set of dots . . . there should be a pause in the narrative so that you can really study any images or feelings that come your way and get as much as possible from them. At first the pictures may be blurred and vague, but like remembering dreams, there is a knack to it which you will get with practice. Be patient.

You may find if you share this experience with a friend that he or she sees different things, or senses quite another place. That does not matter. Just as your memory of a shared event will differ, so do people's perception of the scenery of these inner journeys. The images must be based on memory, and if you have never been to the place in which this path was set, the Algarve coast of Portugal, you will have had to invent or recall the nearest thing you have seen. Nowhere in Britain are there cliffs of sandstone the colour of tomato soup, backing a white beach, where the sea, depending on the weather, is grey or blue or emerald green. Create what you can and revel in whatever images you can literally conjure up. That is what matters, for it is widening your own experience. It will also, through delving into memory, uncover aspects of your self that you may have forgotten, and it will brighten your dream life too!

A 'Place Between the Worlds'

It is a good idea to make use of these techniques in ordinary life, for magic can be applied to mundane matters as well as being separate from everyday existence. If you cannot get to sleep, create a visual journey to take you to the Land of Nod. Imagine in great detail a peaceful place, warm and filled with lulling sounds and scents. Try to examine every flower, every object or person there, and you will find it works far better than sleeping tablets. It works on children too, so if they are hard to settle down at night give them a small drink of warm milk and honey, which is nature's own soporific, and tell them a tale of wonder and beauty. Get them to travel into the realms of dreamland and soon they will be asleep, if you speak gently and lull them with your words.

You can also apply this to real places and discover where you left some lost item. Relive any good or bad experience silently in a peaceful place and you will learn a great deal more from it. Even the most unpleasant happenings can be reviewed calmly so that they do not become unhappy events to be left festering in your memory.

In magical lodges the technique of pathworking is often used to lead the whole brotherhood into a shared experience of another place, a sacred temple or centre of the wisdom they seek. All will share the visions, each seeing his or her own interpretation of the images described, and it is in this 'Place between the Worlds' that a magic happening can be translated into a real event.

Re-read old tales, science fiction novels and historical tracts and see to what extent you can enter into the scenes described and participate in the events. You may in this way uncover considerable amounts of fascinating information about different eras, or old heroes or out-of-this-world places. It is a very cheap form of entertainment, ideal for filling any spare moments, and there is no end to the material that can be turned into films to be shown in your personal 'inner theatre'. It will also release mental blockages and make clear the paths of awareness and intuition, which is what living is all about.

5.
GETTING FIT FOR MAGIC

Magic, as you will have come to realize by now, requires certain training and certain disciplines which these days people are expected to be able to apply to their own lives. In the past, the magical schools were run pretty much on the lines of monasteries. Each student was committed from an early age to follow a discipline, rules and patterns of conduct in common with the others. All rose together, worshipped at the same time, dressed alike, ate and worked in unison and none of them needed to make any decisions at all. Now we are living in the wide world with all its choices and personal freedom. In order to get the best out of our magical abilities and grow into the most effective individuals we are capable of becoming, we need to learn self-discipline and control.

The methods of magical training presented here are designed to enlarge the percentage of your life that is under your own direct control and, as your magical skills advance, help you cope with more aspects of both your ordinary pursuits and the large area of your inner life that has been long overlooked. During all the activities in which your state of consciousness is altered, in meditation and the other exercises, you will always have total control. If there is an emergency or something that needs your immediate action, you will be ready to cope, not under the sway of some enchanter, spellbound and helpless. The various skills you gain from these occult studies should make you more able to deal with any situation, because you will have gained awareness, not only of the obvious, but of all the subtle aspects of any experience that are too often missed.

Not only should you find your powers of concentration increase and that you become more relaxed and at peace with the world, but by studying the various methods suggested here you should become totally well and be able to offer healing and comfort to those around you. When you began the exercises, you had to examine the state of your self, acknowledge any faults and failings, and see reflected in the mirror of reality the real you. Perhaps you admitted habits or states of body or mind that were not totally pleasing, or stress situations which you can only deal with by taking drugs. It is important that you try to get your health under your own control too, as well as the inner workings of your mind.

If you suffer some kind of illness or disability, what are you doing about it? Have you consulted a doctor and what was his advice? Have you ever been told that 'Nothing can be done in a case like yours. You will have to live with it. Your problem is due to your age, lifestyle, etc.'? Did you take that advice seriously, and have you given up hope for ever being 100 per cent well? Read on!

Allopathic and Alternative Medicine
The human body is a wonderful creation. It is extremely complex both in design and operation, and the more that is known about its various functions the more incredible it is seen to be. Like anything else, it can go wrong, break down or be damaged. Left to itself, or given the right assistance, it can probably go a long way to putting itself right. We live in an age of 'miracle drugs', 'wonder cures' and so on, but there are lots of troubles that still have no

certain cure. Things like the common cold, depression, certain cancers and many other simple and serious complaints still cannot be innoculated against, or prevented by drugs.

For over a hundred years most people have been treated by allopathic medicine, that is treatment, medical or surgical, which is based on the idea of alleviating the symptoms. If you have a fever it is thought that a drug which brings your temperature down will speed your recovery. If you have a pain it is to be eased with analgesics, and so on. Other forms of treatment have taken a different approach. For example, homoeopathy, which treats like with like, argues that if a body has a fever, it is that body's way of striving to throw off the illness, and so in homoeopathic treatment a drug would be given that causes a fever in a healthy person. In this way the body is aided to act in its own way of curing itself. Homoeopathy and many of the other natural forms of healing use minute doses of drugs, so diluted that traces are hard or even impossible to detect, in the medicine actually taken, of the healing substance. However, these tiny doses are as effective as ordinary medicines and they seldom have any side effects, which are a common occurrence with allopathic drugs.

Many other forms of treatment do not follow the conventional lines of western medicine. Acupuncture, for example, suggests that there are 'meridians' through which the life force flows. If a blockage is made in any one of the fourteen main channels some imbalance and subsequently illness will result. By allowing the life energy to flow freely, often by inserting extremely fine silver or gold needles, or by massage, or by the application of heat, the balance is restored, the pain relieved and the patient recovers. These, and many other forms of treatment, using herbs, diet, flower essences and so on, are called 'alternative therapies', because they are alternatives to conventional allopathic medicine.

If you have not been helped by the usual forms of treatment, or if you suffer from some ailment which is hard to define and describe to an ordinary doctor, you might well benefit from a visit to an alternative therapist. Apart from homoeopaths or herbalists, whose medicines are of herbal or natural elements, mineral or flower essences, there are a number of healers who treat by massage, manipulation of joints, bones or the spine, or who use other methods of 'laying on of hands' or 'spiritual healing'.

Any form of healing that encourages the unwell body to heal itself rather than drugging it or cutting into it unnecessarily has advantages. Although many people dislike the idea of having needles stuck into them, the fine ones used in acupuncture should not hurt if the therapist is skilled. Osteopaths who manipulate bones and ligaments often offer help in cases of long term backache, stiff necks and 'frozen shoulders' and so on. Chiropractors work mainly on the spine and they successfully treat many back, neck and headache problems, as well as complaints which are caused by compression on nerves in the back.

There are also many less easily explained therapies, such as colour healing where the individual or damaged area is flooded with light of a particular colour. Naturopaths rely on the natural abilities of a body to put itself right by recommending a simple, basic diet, plenty of water to bathe in, drink and relax in, so that toxins or poisons in the system may be quickly eliminated. Radionics practitioners use a form of dowsing to pinpoint areas of infection, and use various instruments from simple pendulums to elaborate 'black boxes' both to diagnose and to treat a patient. Although it is not easy to understand *how* such methods may work, they are certainly effective, and a great number of people from all walks of life, suffering from every possible kind of ill health, physical, mental or spiritual, can be helped by some form of therapy. It is also often possible for many people to discover they have healing ability of their own, which can be used to cure their own minor ills and those of people about them. Everyone who seeks to practice magic should at least try to heal by whatever methods they can. Many of the more complicated systems have a simpler form, which can be learned in the way conventional first aid is learned. Common ailments like headaches, stiff muscles, bruises and minor tensions and depressions can all be treated by application of alternative first aid methods, and there are plenty of basic books on all the therapies mentioned above.

Bach Flower Remedies

When you have learned some of the techniques of magic for yourself you may wish to apply them in the field of healing. Everyone has some abilities here, and there are always people in need of sympathetic treatment in your circle of acquaintances. You may study simple forms of herbal medicine; massage; reflexology, which concerns finding areas on a patient's feet which reflect inner blockages or troubles; shiatsu, which is a form of acupuncture without the needles; or any of the more magical treatments. Some of the most useful, because they work in areas which are not tackled by orthodox medicine, are the Bach Flower Remedies.

Dr Edward Bach was a qualified bacteriologist and one day he was sitting in his garden and noticed the petals of a flower had fallen into a glass of water. He wondered if some of the 'virtue', or health-giving strength, of the flower could be transferred into the water and so act as a medicine. Over the years he experimented and discovered thirty-eight different flowers, shrubs or trees which had some healing properties. These do not act directly on physical disorders like fevers or infections, but on 'subtle' mental states, like fear, anguish, nervousness or terror. He was convinced many people suffer on a mental level and this prevents natural healing of bodily ills by their internal balance system.

The Bach Flower Remedies are made by blending flowers with pure spring water in sunshine. A small amount of brandy is added to preserve the virtue. These are effective in the case of many of the uncertainties of life, or where people have been injured or unwell for no particular reason. They help the inner self combat disturbing influences and bring calm and natural healing.

Because they are made of flower extracts they are safe for children and work well on animals or the very old. Like many natural remedies, they do not always work immediately, but they are gentle and cannot cause any side effects. It is necessary to take the recommended dose for a few weeks in some cases, until it brings the inner self back into balance. More information about these remedies and how best to prescribe them comes in a later chapter.

Stop Smoking, by Magic

It is very much in your own interest to get yourself well, and stay that way. Magic is not an easy matter, you will need to be strong and fit to carry the responsibility you take upon yourself when you begin to practice the arts of magic. When you began the survey of your self and the meditations on your name, did you consider any bad habits you have? If you smoke, you must know that inhaling carbon and nicotine and all the other harmful materials is likely to shorten your life, or make you reliant on medicines or surgery to keep you alive. Perhaps you are a tobacco addict, but YOU can cure yourself.

An addiction is the combination of a mental need and a physical desire. Smoking may be soothing, but it is actually numbing your reactions. Because you have poisoned a part of your system it cannot work to get itself, and consequently your whole self, well. You can give up because you are stronger than the part of you that is craving more of the harmful substances. You *can* decide that health is better than illness or early death. You *can* make up your mind that you are going to be in charge of your whole being and not let some chemical dictate what you do with your body and your money. No one wants to be controlled by anyone else, so why should you be ruled by a harmful craving which is making you less than you can be?

It is obviously hard to stop smoking, but it is within your grasp. Imagine yourself strong, healthy and free of this (or any other) bad habit. You see yourself able to cope, as you can, with any unpleasant cravings you may have. You do not need any expensive therapy; you simply throw away the cigarettes in your possession and join the ranks of the non-smokers. You can try cutting down, but that is not a magical act. It is too easy to slide back from thirty to forty, or ten to twenty without noticing. If you give up, that is it. You will be able to really test your magical ability. If you can do this, tackle every unpleasant longing by meditating on getting the poisons out of your system, imagining every breath you take is bringing in healing oxygen and washing out dirty, black tars and harmful chemicals, it will enable you to get a greater hold on your health.

If you find your hands wish for something to play with instead of a cigarette, carry a lump of modelling clay with you to mould into various shapes, or even a nice round pebble to fondle. All the time imagine a breath of healing air filling you. It does not take long for you to discover the taste of foods again, or to smell flowers and sweet incenses. You will notice the unpleasant stench in bars or smokey rooms which never bothered you before, and come to realize why non-smokers dislike it! If you can achieve the freedom to select what you take in, you will also be able to help others. If you have a companion to share your magical exercises with, make sure he or she is smoke-free too. It can be a great relief when you discover you are in control again. Not only will your body appreciate the change, but your intuitive senses, which have also been numbed by addiction, will begin to come into play. If you have lived on nicotine and strong coffee or tea for a long time you will be amazed how the subtler senses re-emerge from their drugged state.

Meditational Bathing

A simple and effective way of getting yourself to feel well is to take a meditational and medicinal bath. This is one time when you ought to be able to consider yourself and see if you are happy with the body you are at present occupying. Run in a nice bathful of hot water, scented perhaps with some fragrant essence, or natural herbs, and without using soap, lie back and consider yourself. Relax and become still, lightly floating, undisturbed and warm, just as you were before you were born. Be honest: are you too fat or too thin? Are you flabby or bulgy with over-developed areas? You are your own problem, but by considering what you are like, and what you might like to become, you can gradually change yourself.

For anyone who just cannot find time to meditate in a conventional way, this can often provide a suitable alternative. By going back into the water, in which element life may well have begun, it is easier to cast off the conventional ties and return to simpler, more basic thoughts and ideas. Allow yourself to be free and immersed in a warm relaxed state when new ideas may come to you. When you are ready to get on with real life you can symbolically wash off all the problems and hindrances to achieving total awareness and control of your life. Watch them depart with the foam down the plug hole and arise, clean not only in body but in spirit. You can actually build a very effective ritual about something as basic as taking a bath, adding scented essence and heat, imagining the steam carrying aloft prayers and ambitions to a level where they can become 'real'.

Natural Eating
As you began by examining the way you felt about yourself and started to come to terms with the 'real' you, you must apply the same sort of examination to the way you eat, and the things you enjoy. If you live entirely on pre-packed 'instant' food it may take a while to re-educate your palate and digestion to accept more natural foods. There are several reasons for suggesting that more attention should be given to eating unprocessed fruit and vegetables, one of which is the necessity of avoiding potentially harmful chemical additives. Another is that a piece of fruit or a raw green plant is probably still filled with its own life force. It will have all its vital vitamins and trace elements unspoiled and these minute natural chemical doses are valuable in balancing a diet.

Some people suggest all magicians should automatically be vegetarians, or better still vegans, who eat no animal products at all. In practice, most of the best-known occultists have eaten meat and other conventional things. What matters is your attitude to what you eat and how you see it as being good for you, not only as a body, but as an 'inner self' too. If you try to eat as many different things as you can, you will be increasing the chance of absorbing all the minute traces of minerals and vitamins you need from natural sources. It is not necessary to indulge in special vitamin supplements or other medicines, except occasionally as a tonic.

Do try to eat raw fruits and vegetables each day. Children will benefit far more from a slice of sweet apple, pear or banana or a piece of carrot or celery than a chocolate bar. If you wish to lose weight, one of the best things you can do is to make a large bowl of mixed chopped vegetables and fruits and nibble it all day. Avocado pears are an excellent source of vegetable protein and often the small ones are cheap. Red and green peppers have plenty of vitamin C, fennel adds a spicy taste to a salad, kohl rabi makes a change from carrots as a hot vegetable. Aubergines, courgettes and peppers stewed with some garlic or onions in tomato juice make an interesting thick soup or toast-topper, especially with a little cheese grilled until runny.

Be adventurous in eating, because it can be a real treat to discover you really like the taste of some strange objects which you had previously not dared to try. Ladies fingers added to stew give an oriental touch, kiwi fruits sliced over a mixture of sliced pears, bananas and apples make a far healthier fruit salad than the sickly sweet tinned variety. Cut down on white sugar and if you need sweetness try dark brown natural sugar, or thin honey.

You can exchange some of your cups of tea or coffee for either a glass of natural fruit juice or even one of the sparkling spring waters that are appearing on many supermarket shelves now. Change soft white bread for one of the wholemeal or granary-type loaves, for these are far more nutritious and contain fibre which keeps your system in healthy order. Try plain boiled rice, white or brown, instead of chips, or fill up with wholewheat spaghetti or noodles. Again, go on a voyage of discovery around your local supermarket or healthfood shop. The different items need not be expensive and many of the beans, lentils and varieties of rice or noodles prove cheaper as you use less per portion because they are filling.

There is a traditional British dish called a Salmagundi, which is a huge dish covered with an elaborate design made up of all sorts of vegetables and fruits with slices of hardboiled eggs, anchovies, cooked meat or fish and olives etc. This makes an interesting centerpiece to a party and can keep a family fed for several days. The base is usually chopped white cabbage with patterns of sliced tomato, cooked potatoes, raw carrot, celery, beetroot, green and red peppers, chicory, watercress, raw spinach and onion rings. This can also have slices of apple (dipped in lemon juice so they stay white,) peaches, mangoes, oranges, pineapple and grapes scattered about. It may sound very strange, but the combination of fruits and vegetables is pleasing to the palate, and the various new items will add a sparkle.

Try to experiment every day. Greek humus or taramasalata eaten with flat pitta bread makes a change from beans on toast; try French ratatouille instead of soup as a starter; a half small melon filled with fresh strawberries is better than a tin of peaches in syrup. Open your eyes to interesting things and do not be put off because they look strange.

Do not ignore the wild fruits and herbs which grow all over the country too. The blackberries, whortles and rosehips found in country lanes can provide a free basis for pies, jams or wines. All contain valuable natural elements and the outdoor effort of collecting them brings you closer to nature and the seasons of the year. Many farms now have 'pick your own fruit' sessions and a sunny afternoon gathering fresh strawberries or raspberries or blackcurrants can be extremely rewarding.

You might think the above has very little to do with magic, yet by working hand in hand with nature you will be experiencing the great rite of creation in all its season-long splendour. Magic is not something that has to be locked away in the dark. It lives under the sun and all around you where plants grow, where springs flow and where stars dance in the zenith of heaven.

Magic is concerned with living to the full, and if you can strive to be well, to eat sensibly and adventurously you will start to become a far more effective human being. Once you start to feel fitter, you will find your subtle senses or intuitions will begin to start to function. You will be able to 'feel' how things are, or what needs to be done. Your meditations will begin to fill you with ideas and inspiration and each day you will feel more able to cope, more flexible and more alive. It does take hard work, dedication and patience, but surely such a gift is worth it? No one else can get you healthy and fit if you will not make the effort yourself, and in a changing world it is far better to be in charge and control of any changes that are happening to you. Look in the mirror, and then in the food cupboard, and see where you can change things now!

6.
THE EXPERIENCE
OF RELIGION

Every major religion once had its mysteries, its magical and secret side. In some cases this has been lost and with it the power of that faith to attract and hold adherents. This has done nothing to prevent new cults appearing, but the trouble with cults is that they interpose a leader, teacher or guru between the seeker and that which he is seeking.

The view most practising occultists hold is that there is a Creator; that angelic forces or gods and goddesses can be contacted in a variety of ways, and that prayers or ritual invocations can bring real and genuine answers. The adherents of many religions look forward with the confidence of faith to some future state, but for those who cannot accept the idea of a deity there can be no concept of an afterlife: their actions must be directed towards making the most of the here and now. The magician does not believe: he knows that his prayers can be answered. He has seen or sensed the presence of angels or the gods, and he has had a variety of real personal experiences. He is aware that direct contact can be made between himself and the powers he works with.

Because this experience is personal to the magician there can be no common formula that applies to everyone. There has to be complete freedom so that every student can come to terms with his own concept of God, the gods or no God. Like experiments in other branches of magical practice, it will be necessary for you to meditate, consider and perhaps walk a path of imagination that will lead you to have some religious experiences of your own. There can be no rights and wrongs or religious belief any more than there can be absolute rules about the job you have or the pattern of life you lead. You must seriously consider the question in the light of your current knowledge, experiment, and later experience things for yourself.

Some religions teach that suffering is a necessary part of life, that sacrifices have to be made, that sins will be punished. Certainly life does have the habit of throwing nasty experiences our way and from them we do indeed learn; but does that get us any closer to heaven? Probably not. On the other hand, there are some modern organizations with eastern leaders that teach another path: that life is joy, that we have freedom in order to be free, that we can love and live as well as possible. Life can be joyous; it can be filled with wonderful experiences and beautiful relationships, but we need to work at it. We need to cast off the shackles that have been laid upon us by the society in which we live, examine everything and judge things for ourselves. It is not necessary to cast away everything from the past, cut ourselves off from all the good and bad events we have experienced and the lessons they have taught us; we must simply examine each concept carefully and evaluate it for ourselves. Much of the information we have gathered about how we ought to live is valuable and still true, but when it has been held under the spotlight of new understanding it may be found to be even more valuable. It is wrong to cast out all teachings and religious attitudes and dismiss holy books and holy men as irrelevant, ineffective, or worse. Each should be studied, and then, perhaps, cast aside.

The Mother Figure

Many aspects of modern occult work, as seen from the outside, have a strong religious bias. Witchcraft, for example, is closely associated in many books with the Old Religion, the pagan faith of the people before Christianity took hold. The Old Religion is concerned with nature, with the changing seasons seen as the life story of a God and Goddess. Through the centuries these have had many names and different personalities. They have been publicly worshipped and held in awe in many parts of the world. The God and the Goddess appear disguised somewhat in most modern faiths. The Lady of the pagans is the Virgin Mary, the Bride which the Sabbath awaits in the Jewish faith.

The idea that there is a female aspect to God is a very ancient one. The earliest artefacts to be identified as having religious significance show a female figure, greatly pregnant and fat with milk. She is the Earth Mother, the bringer forth of new life, the symbol of fertility and generation. The function of the mother was known long before the part played by the father was recognised. Many ancient societies were ruled by women and the inheritance of land was through the mother.

The bearing of children must have seemed a magical act, and even today there are places women visit if they wish to bear a child. The Old Religion was concerned with fertility, because without an ample harvest of crops, livestock and children a primitive village would soon die. The need for a good supply of natural resources has been paramount to the evolution of any society, group or country. It is still true, for if oil, coal and natural gas all gave out we would not survive long. All these things are the gifts of nature, long ago worshipped as Mother Nature, the great creatrix of all life.

Animus and Anima

Today people are dissatisfied with conventional religions because they do not appeal to the inner self. The soul is left hungry and this leads to yearnings that are hard to identify. People feel unloved, unfulfilled and empty, even though they often have good homes, comfortable incomes and all the benefits of twentieth-century living. Something is missing. Dr Carl Jung, the psychologist who advanced the study of the human mind in far more ways than is usually appreciated, wrote a book called *Modern Man in Search of a Soul.* Jung was convinced that as well as satisfying our bodily needs, we had a soul that had to be tended as well. If this spirit is left alone and ignored it has ways of making its presence felt, and perhaps lies at the root of many forms of 'mental illness'. Many of these seem to be sicknesses of the spirit, the depression, the divided-self of schizophrenia, the anger and confusion of manic depressives, the feeling of threat or danger felt by many phobics. Perhaps it is the forgotten spirit trying to make contact looking over the shoulder, leaning on the individual and causing depression by its own sense of isolation.

Jung said that each individual has an inner self of the opposite sex. If we can come to terms with these inner parts of ourselves we shall have a much better understanding of other people and what makes them act as they do. This is another subject that requires further reading, careful thought and consideration. Many of Jung's ideas, based on his study of people, of alchemy and the Eastern divination system called the *I Ching* (the Book of Changes), are accepted by open-minded occultists and magicians.

No one should feel it necessary to accept the idea of a goddess or a god as a personification of a super-human being if this concept has no appeal for them, but it is well worth studying some of the many books on ancient religions that tell the legends of Isis and Osiris, of the Indian Gods and Goddesses, and of the pantheons of Greek and Roman deities to see how you feel about them. In the past, instead of believing in a single male God many cultures worshipped a variety of gods and goddesses, each of whom had particular speciality or 'job'. There was a god of war and a goddess of wisdom, one god concerned

with expansion and growth, another with communic-
ations, travel and trickery. Many of the gods were linked
with heavenly bodies, the Sun and Moon, and the planets,
whose names are those of the Roman gods and goddesses,
Venus, Mars, Jupiter, Saturn and Mercury. Later discoveries, like Neptune, Pluto and Uranus, still have the
names of ancient gods.

Dion Fortune, who wrote many books on all aspects of
magic, wrote in her occult novel *The Sea Priestess*: 'All
Gods are One God, and All Goddesses are One Goddess,
and there is One Initiator.' This is a useful way of
understanding that there can be aspects of God that need
a separate name or title, yet beneath all the variety there
was one Creator, one source from which life, the universe
and everything sprang. The words of the Bible tell us that
'God created man in his own image'; yet another translation states that 'God created man in his imagination':
again we are back to the magical power of image making.
By imagining the gods and goddesses as they are described
in classical literature, or shown in Egyptian wall paintings,
you are recreating them. Like Tinkerbell, the fairy in
J.M. Barrie's *Peter Pan,* they have to be believed in or
experienced or they will fade away. If you believe in a
Goddess of Love and create her in your heart, you must
gain in the ability to give out love. If you create a God of
Plenty, surely you will grow in benefits from that source.
When you need a particular sort of help you can either
rediscover an old deity with an appropriate function, or
design a new one – an up-to-date image to help you
achieve your wish. It is a way in which man and the gods
have worked in partnership for a long time, and is still
effective.

The God and the Goddess
The most basic forms of the God and Goddess that occur
in many modern rituals are concerned with the powers
traditionally associated with the Sun and the Moon. The
Sun God has many names like Helios, Apollo, and Sol,
and the Goddess, who reflects the varying phases of the
Moon, often has three different names: Diana, the new

moon maiden, Artemis, the full moon mother, and Hecate, the waning moon crone. Most of the classical religions had this idea of three Goddesses and one God who took several roles during the course of the natural year. At one time he might be the lover of the Goddess, her father, or her son. In the West a complicated story is told and enacted each year about this relationship of Earth and Sky, or Sun and Moon.

Many of the legends of heroes and heroines are really versions of this annual myth, retold as if they were the actions of real historic people. Sometimes the stories of the Old Gods have become so interwoven into the legends that the characters are thought of as actual kings who lived in historic time. One familiar one is the story of King Arthur. History places him as a leader of a band of warriors who fought against the Saxon invaders in about the 6th century AD, but legends place him much earlier. His court and adventures mix real conflicts with traditional tasks that the Sun God as hero was called upon to undertake. The magical sword, the wizard Merlin, who directs and guides the young king until he is enchanted by a witch, the perfect knights, the beautiful ladies and the quest for the Holy Grail blend history and myth.

The quest for the Holy Grail can also be seen as a quest for the true self, and the adventures the legendary knights encountered will be found to occur in the lives of all seekers. There is a Sun God, who is born at the dead of winter, soon after the solstice, who grows with each passing day, and who receives his sword and arrows from his Mother, the ever-virgin Goddess. Later, as the year turns, he becomes her lover and when she is disguised as a deer, he chases her into the forest. At midsummer he is at his height and fights the dark side of himself, the winter king. He loses, and later on, as the spirit of the corn, is laid low at harvest. The Earth Goddess receives him and takes him into her house. This is still symbolized by the corn dolly, made from the last sheaf of standing corn. Autumn brings the bonfires of Hallowe'en, Summer's End, when the whole family gathered and invited the Goddess and the God, who were their ancestors, to visit the house.

Traditionally, on this ghostly eve all the dead return to join the revels, and the unborn children meet their parents in spirit. As the king of winter, the God at his lowest ebb rules with the dark queen, Lady of Night, and at midwinter he is born again, a weak child, the star child, the bringer of hope in a time of darkness.

These legends form part of the ritual pattern of many of the modern covens of witches, with the high priest and priestess acting out the story of the God and Goddess. The Druids follow this cycle, and many other pagans, whose ceremonies are less well known, also work their way through the stories of the old gods, just as the Christian Church tells different stories from the Bible at each feast.

The Old Religion and its current adherents are all seekers after joy. It is a religion of personal experience and of ceremonies that bring companionship and happiness to the people who share them. They do not see the cakes and wine of their communion as the blood and body of a slain god, but as tokens of the harvest from the Earth Mother and her Lord. There should be no idea of sacrifice for the corn is grown to be harvested, the fruit trees are cultivated to provide a store of winter food. No one can offer anything except himself, and it is his life of service to the cause of Life that is offered. Killing animals or offering cut flowers is a strange idea when it is to the Life Force that these are being offered.

It is hard to explain how a student of magic should go about coming to terms with the Lord and Lady of Life, and except by experiencing communion with them you cannot judge their reality for yourself. The best way to go about it is to devise a place that is not entirely in our world nor entirely in theirs, and in this half-way-house, meet them face to face. It is another application of imagination, but you will frequently be guided as to how the images or feelings should be shaped. Like the other exercises, you will need a quiet time and place, and if you already have some idea of symbols for the God and Goddess, it might be appropriate to place these where you can see them without effort.

You will need to build up an image of the sort of place you imagine them to inhabit. If you choose to meet one of the classical gods of ancient Greece or Egypt, you may wish to construct a temple after the manner of the area. If you feel the gods are part of nature, then you might imagine a wild moor, rocky mountain or deserted sea shore, a glade in a forest or an island at the centre of a sacred lake. If you find it hard to describe a setting, you may find some poems may inspire you, or perhaps descriptions of sacred places taken from books. If you cannot imagine gods in human form, visualize them as powers. For example, you could see a landscape in daytime. You could start from sunrise, in a bare winter landscape. As the sun rises, its life-giving power turns the fields green; the corn and other plants begin to grow. When the heat of noon has passed and the sun begins to set, the corn is ripened and is ready for harvest. Here you will be seeing the real effect of sunlight on growing things without personifying the power of the sun.

The same applies to the moon. Her light can guide the lost in midnight's darkness. She also reflects the changing nature of women and, as she rules the sea, she affects the body, which contains a great deal of water. The moon actually alters the moods of many people, bringing periods of lucid dreams, visions or greater psychic sensitivity. You can imagine the three separate Goddesses, the maid, mother and old woman, each teaching you things; or just see her as a barren globe, circling our home planet. If you imagine a dark night with the sky lit by many stars, and then allow whichever phase of the moon you wish to work with to flood that darkness with silvery light, you will begin to sense her effect upon you.

In each case, create a flexible image through which the God or Goddess can show aspects of themselves to you. Some people are rather frightened by the idea of seeing these great powers face to face; yet it is an experience which ought to be sought out since it adds a new dimension to your understanding of life. Any fears you may have are reflections of your own inner uncertainty. The gods will not harm us, and often a closer understanding of the powers which they represent can result from exercises or meditations. These powers can help us in many aspects of our daily lives, and there is nothing to fear from them. Do not be afraid to venture into the realm of the gods, or draw back from creating a safe place in which to meet them, for they represent a great power for creativity and growth, and through understanding them we can rediscover innate inner strengths. In the Gnostic Mass, each communicant, taking the cake and wine, says: 'There is no part of me which is not of the Gods.' That, too, is worth thinking about. We are parts of creation just as the trees or the stars are; but we are able to grow and set ourselves free to experience a wide range of things, if we so wish.

Perhaps the easiest way to think about the God and the Goddess is to see them as forces for CHANGE. They change the weather from cold, spring rain to hot mid-summer sunshine, the growth of plants from dead-seeming seeds to flowering, fruiting and seeding trees and shrubs. It is the power of change which turns the tiny, helpless baby gradually into the full-grown, competent adult. Change too, has led to the evolution of dust into planets, chemical elements into simple life forms, and, aided by the Great Initiator, has changed lifeless matter into all the variety of species of plants, animals, birds and insects that inhabit our planet. There is some tiny spark of the Creator in every part of creation, from the simplest amoeba to the largest tree, from the most complicated animal to the loftiest mountain. Nothing is without its own God-given life force, and through our sharing of this tiny spark of the eternal we are able to work with it through magic making, healing and understanding far beyond our own abilities.

Reincarnation
Another aspect of this divine spark in man is that it is immortal and does not die when our body does. The doctrine of reincarnation holds that each soul lives through many human lifetimes, gradually gaining skills and strengthening its power to evolve. We recognize this

eternal factor within us and probably think of it as our
'selves'. As the soul lives each life on earth it gains new
experiences and balances the pattern, becoming more
complete. Between lives it rests, in a state which might be
thought of as 'heaven'. Here it can assess its own progress
and is not 'judged' or made to account for 'sins' but can
see dispassionately how it has done in life. If a certain part
of its development has been overlooked it will come back
into life to learn the lessons so far omitted. This may
account for geniuses, young children who can 'remember
being someone else', and early skills.

There is a good deal of research going on into this
subject at the present time, and there are large numbers
of books being published, both about the concept of
reincarnation and the methods by which anyone can
explore their own past. It is important to recognize that
though a soul may have experienced many lives and
deaths these would not always be among the privileged
classes of the time. There are many accounts of people
recalling being pharaohs, priests, kings, people of high
rank or historical significance, rather than humble servants, farmhands, soldiers and slaves. They seem to forget
that a simple life can teach lessons that are just as
important — being a parent, coping in hard times, being
persecuted, ill-used and suffering disease and neglect.
Most of humanity has had periods of striving to raise itself
up, and times when nature was against it — times of
drought, plague and famine. Although suffering is not
thought to be necessary, as is taught in some major faiths,
it does bring out aspects of the human soul which might
otherwise lie unexploited.

If you do want to explore your own past lives do go
about it sensibly because it can be an unsettling experience. It is vital to have a reliable companion, plenty of
time, and to make detailed records. You may be very
frightened, for by accepting reincarnation you already
acknowledge that you have died and been reborn. Death
is not an easy subject to deal with and many deaths in
earlier centuries are likely to have been violent, painful
and nasty! Do not take everything you learn without

checking the facts — there are plenty of accurate hisorical accounts of most times and places, and the research can help confirm whether what you recall is valid and 'real', or just fantasy or imagination, or worst of all, created to flatter your ego!

Karma

Central to the idea of reincarnation is the doctrine of Karma, which is a cyclical concept of action and reaction. It is sometimes thought that it is simply a way for one individual to pay another back for harm done in a past lifetime, but it is far more complex than that. If you were killed by A in a past life and encounter him again in another incarnation, it does not mean that you have to kill him in order to get the balance right. Often there is some other way in which you and he work out the karma you share. Perhaps he repays the debt in some other way, for his death at this time might not be right Sometimes it can be seen that your previous death was 'due', and that there was no blame to be dispensed; there could even have been an earlier life in which you caused A's death. Without a great deal of digging it is hard to get to the bottom of a single event, and life is full of the effect of karma.

It is sometimes thought that crippling diseases are karmic debts being paid off, for individuals may have maimed, tortured or crippled others in the past and are now suffering for their cruelty. No one knows if this is true, but karma does teach lessons, and good and bad deeds may well be balanced out. You must remember, though, that it is the soul that chooses the conditions into which it will be born each time. No other being directs the pattern of reincarnation. It is also possible that long-lasting relationships can continue from one life to the next. Often you will meet people for the first time yet you recognize them and even find you become close friends; you feel as if you have 'been there before' when visiting somewhere new, or occasionally take an instant dislike to someone, for no reason. You feel sympathy or antipathy towards strangers, sense bonds of love or hate which seem to linger beyond death and through great spans of time.

It is important that the bonds of love should outlive the grave and it is these that all religions should teach their followers to construct. If you can give out love, to God or the gods, to mankind, to those closely related to you, as well as to casual acquaintances it will be reflected back on you and you will be loved. Be prepared to show love, not in a 'sloppy' way, but genuinely from the heart. Touch people lovingly, cuddle those closest to you, put your arm around someone in sympathy, support the elderly. Be open, unembarrassed and easy with those around you, and it will be repaid immediately by a happier, more loving atmosphere. 'God is Love', it is written, and all of us have a spark of God in us. Let it shine as a flame of love, warming all our relationships. You will be surprised what a little love can do.

7.
DIVINATION:
STRETCHING YOUR SENSES

If you have made a serious effort to master the earlier exercises you will have begun to realize that there is a great deal that you had not known about yourself before, and perhaps you are also finding new skills. Divination is another magical art requiring study and practice, but there are forms of it anyone can learn. Technically, 'divination' means communing with the Divinity, and thus receiving information that would otherwise be unavailable. There are all sorts of methods of divination using symbols, like the Tarot cards; there are the hexagrams of the *I Ching*; the configurations of the astrological birth chart; the visions 'seen' in a crystal ball; the interpretation of tea leaves; palmistry; graphology (the art of analysing handwriting). Some methods are very simple — for example, using the nine symbols of divining stones, sometimes called rune stones. Originally, rune stones had characters from the old Scandinavian alphabets on them.

Again, there are dozens of excellent books dealing with each of these methods. Always consult several books on the same subject of divination because every author has his own ideas and interpretations, and there is no 'one' correct way. Do look at a number of different methods as you will find some immediately 'click' and make sense; others take longer to reveal what they can tell you.

The Tarot

Each of the 78 cards of the traditional Tarot pack has a specific meaning, and every combination with the other cards around it tells a different story. It is only by becoming familiar with the images on the deck you use, and letting it 'speak' to you, that you become able to turn a bare mechanical reading of what a book on Tarot says into a valid and thorough reading. This does come with practice. It is also helped by the methods of meditation and visualization which, with the altered state of consciousness that is a part of those techniques, provide a frame of mind that is open to subtle impressions. If you go about any sort of reading coldly and using only the intellect, the result will be shallow and vague. If you relax, you will sink into a perceptive state and open your inner self to receive guidance. This is not a trance state, and trances (when you are no longer in control) are never used in modern occult work of any sort. You simply attend to what the symbols have to say rather than to what is going on in the room about you.

Often you are giving a reading for another person and to some extent you will be turning your attention to their life. It is possible, whilst in a meditative state, to perceive clearly the way that the symbols explain themselves. A Tarot card depicting a scene of struggle might be seen in terms of a person striving to gain a better understanding of the question, or it could be his attempts to succeed in his job, or even an actual quarrel among his companions. The same applies to the positions of planets in a person's horoscope: read in one way, they could mean strengths and successes in the world; in another, difficulties and conflicts inside the individual.

One of the easiest ways to learn what the Tarot cards mean to you is to take cards at random and simply relax, allowing the image to flow through your mind. Jot down what it seems to be saying to YOU — which is far more important than what the same image may have said to the writer of a book. Work through the whole pack until they are all familiar. This method of building your own interpretation is far quicker than trying to learn, parrot fashion, the meanings of cards given by someone else. Everyone is different, everyone has a unique understanding of the world, and that is what is important. Carry the cards about with you, glancing at the odd one whenever you get a chance so that they become easy to recognize. Sometimes they will speak to you, giving information as to what is about to occur.

It is important to realize that divination, no matter what form you may be using, can only indicate one of many possible futures. Life is like a chess game. Each time a move is made, all sorts of other possible moves become available. Life is the same: change one tiny aspect and the whole future pattern could be radically altered. It is in this way that will can be used to overcome or avoid ill luck. If you make up your mind that you will cope with any problem, or change yourself so that the person to whom the misfortune would have befallen is now no longer you, it can be avoided. Remember, man has free will; he can choose what path he takes, and if he learns to use common sense, looking ahead at what may befall, he can walk a much straighter, safer path through life. He has the ability to make decisions about what he wants to happen and mould himself into the person to whom those things will happen.

Do not be afraid to face all the images of the Tarot. Just because there is a card called DEATH, it does not imply the immediate demise of either you or the person you are reading for. It stands for a change, and any change can be for the better. It signifies the end of an era and the start of a new one. The other so-called unlucky cards are generally thought to be the Lightening-Struck Tower and the Devil, but both of these offer a choice. On the one hand, God is striking the tower and as we are all well aware, there are many situations over which we have little control; but usually there is a benefit when the upheaval is over and things look brighter. Do not be afraid to face losing things; it is only a form of growing up when the 'toys' of your previous self are outgrown and put aside. The Devil can often refer to the inner side of your nature, which is wild and uncontrolled. It may be the 'psychic dustbin' of repressed fears and bad habits that has not been tackled and cleared out. It can suggest ill health, but it can equally act as a warning and tell you to do something about the state of your body in time to prevent the trouble actually affecting you. Most cards, and the hexagrams of the I Ching, are concerned with changes because that is when we get opportunities to make things better and alter them to suit our own purposes. As you grow magically, you will be better able to enjoy and control changes in your life, and gain more than you lose.

Like most magical arts this is a complicated and lengthy study, but the sooner you begin the quicker you will be able to get results that give you valuable guidance or information. Be patient; get used to the system you have chosen and work hard to master it. You can apply the techniques of magical ritual to divination as well.

When you go on to the techniques of setting up an altar and a magical circle, which provides a still area free from distractions to mind or spirit, you can make a greater use of the Tarot. To begin with you may feel rather embarrassed when trying to explain the meanings of cards to other people, and it is a good idea to get used to this before you set up as a Monsieur Magicko or Madame Mysterioso who 'Sees all, tells all'. Practise explaining the cards or what they point to on tape until it is easy to give a clear picture of what is going through your head. Draw cards at random and explain the meanings and implications of them until you can make a story that hangs together and that is coherent and informative. If the cards say nothing, which they do from time to time, say so. Honesty is the most important aspect of divination. If the Gods choose to tell you anything it is up to you, on your honour, to pass it on intact and unaltered. If the indications are unlucky, find a way of explaining them so that the questioner understands that things may not go well; but do not send him away quaking in his shoes, certain that the end of the world is nigh.

Never boast about your abilities to divine, or claim to be a fortune teller. If you are asked to predict the outcome of some action, or how a certain plan is likely to work out, be humble. Offer to try to see what might happen, but do not be dogmatic or promise 100 per cent results. No one can do that, for sometimes the voices are dumb, the cards dead and the symbols meaningless. You will only gain a good reputation in this field if you are discreet; do not tell one questioner what you have divined for another, and do not brag about your successes, or these may be the last you enjoy.

Dowsing

Although dowsing is a very ancient art many people do not realize that it is something most of them can learn. Like playing a musical instrument, it takes understanding and practice. In the old days it was usual to use a twig cut from a hazel tree or willow in the shape of a 'Y'. This was held in a rather awkward-seeming grip by the ends of the top of the Y, so that the hands were held palm up, with the thumbs facing outwards. The fingers were lightly curled round the ends of the twig and slight tension was put upon it by tucking in the elbows to the sides and getting the finger knuckles to point forwards. Because the twig was under strain, any tiny movement made by the muscles of the hands or arms would be magnified and the ends of the twig would point sharply up or down. A dowser would walk over a field and when he crossed an underground spring the twig would react. Something in him recognized the unseen water; this made his muscles twitch and the stick showed this clearly. No one is sure how this reaction comes about, but many dowsers make a reliable living, finding not only water, either as a spring or in a pipe, but also tracing electrical wires, gas pipes, sewers, buried treasure and archaeological artefacts.

Nowadays, instead of the twig many dowsers use two metal rods, often made from wire coat hangers. These are cut to give a short end, usually inserted into some sort of tube, and a long arm, about twelve to fifteen inches long. The rods are bent into a right angle and held so that they can swing freely inside the tubes. By gripping the tubes lightly and holding the long arms parallel with the ground, it is possible to walk slowly forwards over an area where hidden minerals or water is suspected. The rods will swing gently in and out but as the dowser crosses the hidden object they will usually swing firmly across one another, and will only uncross when the far side of the stream or pipeline is crossed. This feels very weird at first, and it often seems that the dowser must be cheating; but experiments have been carried out under controlled conditions that clearly demonstrate the dowser is reacting to something he cannot 'know' is there. You can make some of these rods or even buy some specially made ones, and try walking about in your own garden. If you relax and allow the rods to swing freely you will soon begin to notice they seem to react to something. You can help by running a tap to ensure a flow of water, or even walk up to a bucket of water, until you get the hang of it. Like meditation, there is a definite 'knack' which has to be learned. Once you can do it, you only need practice to become adept.

The Pendulum
Another application of the dowsing principle is divination with a pendulum. For this you will need a large bead, small plumb-bob or similar symmetrical object with a hole through it, and about eighteen inches of thin cord, twine or thread. The best sort is woven rather than twisted, as it will not unravel as you use it. Picture cord is ideal as it is thin, cheap and, being an artificial fibre, will not wear out quickly. Once you have threaded the weight onto the cord hold it lightly over the top of your finger so that the pendulum can swing freely in all directions. Just relax your hand and do not make any deliberate movements with it. The first objective is to establish a code which is personal to you. Some books suggest a particular swing means a particular thing but this does not work for

everyone, so establish your own signs. Ask yourself a question to which the answer is 'Yes' – anything simple, like 'Is my name...?' You will soon find the bob begins to move, either in a straight line towards you and away, or left-right, or perhaps in a circle. Ask it to indicate more clearly if the movement is faint and unclear. Keep on with positive questioning until you have a definite movement, than ask a question to which the answer is 'No'. See what the pendulum does then. It ought to be different from the first answer. Again keep on until you have a clear movement which is easily distinguishable from the 'Yes' answer. Ask another 'Yes' question to test the method and then another 'No' question, alternating and allowing the pendulum to swing at least a couple of inches to make its answer clear. Everyone can get some sort of swing going, but sometimes it is a very weak response. You can improve this by changing to the hand you use least. Often the left hand of right-handed people will give very large swings. Unless you get a definite 'Yes' and 'No' swing, which you can tell apart, you will not be able to use the pendulum for some of the magical methods.

Your code for yes and no, or positive and negative, is a way in which the inner you can make a simple communication with the outer self. The inner you has a great many more 'senses' than your outer five. It can detect underground water, lost objects, metal pipes, and less obvious things like 'ley lines', which are ancient power lines apparently linking ancient monuments, stone circles and megalithic structures. (These places are thought to have beneficial magical connections, and are often used for rituals and seasonal festival celebrations where possible.) The use of a pendulum also has many magical applications. For example, if you were reading the Tarot cards for someone and could not decide if a card was relevant or not, by holding a pendulum over it you would get a positive or negative decision. You can use this method to select cards for a reading for yourself, looking at those over which the bob gives a 'Yes' swing. You may use the pendulum as a way of answering any questions to which the answer is yes or no, or if you can develop some sort of binary code with it, for any other purpose. You can sometimes get answers from your inner self to questions your outer self cannot answer.

Healing with the Pendulum

Probably the most important area of divination with a pendulum is that of healing. There might seem to be no obvious connection, but once you realize that everyone has some sort of healing skill, even if they are not yet trained, you will see how the pendulum can be used both to help in diagnosis and in treatment. There is a field of healing called 'Radionics', which uses the same idea as divination to treat all sorts of health problems, both physical and mental, and even things which affect the subtle aspects of the individual, his psychological state or soul. By divining with a 'Black Box', which has dials and magnets inside, it is possible to discover a 'rate' for an illness. Each dial has numbers around it and by slowly turning these in a set fashion whilst stroking a pad of soft rubber it has been found by diviners that the finger will suddenly stick to the pad when a certain number is reached. A similar method of rubbing to reach an answer has been used by wise men in Africa for generations. There, a wooden carved figure, damped with water or spittal, is rubbed with a special block whilst questions are asked. When a particular answer is relevant the block will stick quite definitely to the rubbing figure. The same happens with the Radionics machine. It will suddenly stick and indicate a specific number for each illness.

A more simple method can be used by anyone who has the desire to try to heal or give help to people. First it is necessary to establish if you can actually offer them help, which is done by asking the pendulum 'Can I help this person?' You should get a clear 'Yes', or 'No'. If the answer is negative, then you should suggest the person goes elsewhere for help, rather than try something and get out of your depth. If the anser is 'Yes', you can begin a series of questions. (It is worth bearing in mind that a pendulum can suddenly change the code it is using, especially if you are dealing with a person of the opposite sex, so ask a check question before you go on to lengthy answers.)

Ask things like 'Could an ordinary doctor help?' 'Should this person go into hospital?' 'Is the illness in his/her body, mind, or spirit?' 'Does he/she need magical healing?' 'Can he/she cure himself?' 'If so, how?' and so on. Try to find out from the person what sort of treatment he has tried before, how effective it was, and whether he has sought professional advice.

If you have studied herbal, homoeopathic or even the Bach remedies (which work to alleviate many mental and anxiety states better than anything) you can dowse down a list of methods of treatment. This will help you tune in to the best way of treating the individual. Often a person can go a long way to getting himself right with a little help or guidance from a friend. A change of diet, reduction of bad habits, more controlled relaxation or exercise can often go a long way towards a total cure and involves no drugs or other treatment at all. Foot massage ('Reflexology' or 'Zone Therapy') might be worth learning because it is fairly simple and very effective in all sorts of troubles.

There are thirty-eight Bach remedies, made from the flowers, buds or leaves of various plants or trees, all but one native to Britain. Each treats a particular fear, anxiety, or nervous state. Even long-standing problems can be gradually alleviated by these gentle medicines. It is sometimes difficult to obtain a complete picture, and thus prescribe the best remedy. When this happens it is best to consult your pendulum. First make sure that it is in your power to help the person, and (just as importantly) that the person wishes you to help. If he is at a distance you can still help him, so long as he wishes it. If you can get a clipping of hair, or his signature on a letter or even a clean tissue to which he has put his tongue, you will have a 'witness', a link. This is very important as you are using a magical art and links between the magician/healer and patient are vital to the work. You can use herbal methods to treat animals in the same way.

Often dowsing will show aspects of the case that are not apparent to a non-magical approach. Illnesses are seldom simply caused by a single factor; rather, they are the cumulation of a variety of conditions and dis-eases. We are all surrounded by bacteria and viruses, some of which live inside us and cause no trouble, but when some part of our protective system of health breaks down, for whatever reason, we become susceptible to illness. The less orthodox methods can often reveal the true causes of illness and disease, which may be psychological as much as physical. By treating the *individual* rather than the disease, it is more likely a permanent cure can be found.

Dowsing can help pinpoint allergic reactions to foods or to environmental factors such as pollen. You can often dowse over the body of an unwell person, allowing the pendulum to answer the question: 'Is there anything wrong with this part?' You will sometimes find the area indicated by the pendulum is quite separate from the painful place or the apparent seat of infection; but by looking at the meridians along which acupuncture points lie, you may well find that the pendulum is indicating an unbalanced meridian. Use common sense and build up your skill with a pendulum, or any other form of divination equipment by becoming certain that the answers you perceive are correct at that moment. If you get vague answers, or no clear indications, go back to the basic exercises, play 'treasure hunt' with coins hidden under a carpet by a friend, or work with lists of appropriate questions with answers that can easily be checked.

Most children can dowse and they enjoy playing at finding hidden treasure, or identifying a series of different metals, etc., hidden under a blanket. It makes an original party game to get them searching for concealed prizes. It is possible to hold the pendulum in one hand and point with the other, asking 'Is it hidden in this direction?' The swing will become positive when you point in the right direction. This can also be used out of doors, to locate an underground stream, some lost object or the layout of an archaeological site, for example. Try out as many of these applications of practical divination as you can, for they stretch your senses and improve your magical skills.

Crystal Gazing

Crystal gazing, or scrying, is basically an extension of the art of meditation, but instead of a phrase or subject on which you meditate you use something on which to concentrate your eyes, leaving your mind to range freely. Although a glass or a real crystal ball (very rare these days) is an ideal speculum, a bowl of water, a mirror, or a piece of polished black glass, jet or even coal, will do just as well. A simple and effective 'black mirror' can be made from the glass face from an old alarm clock painted with several coats of matt black paint on the convex side. This should be set in a shallow tin or box, lined with velvet, to make a dull frame around the dark glass. Relax, as you would for meditation, but keep your eyes focused just below the surface of the glass. After a while, when you get into the properly relaxed and altered state, you will find what looks like drifts of mist or smoke begin to form, which gradually thicken and swirl. From this stage, if you remain alert yet very still, you will find the mist begins to clear and pictures, letters, symbols or figures may be seen in the space. It takes a good deal of practise to get to this stage, for it often happens that the surprise of seeing the formation of the mist or smoke disturbs the relaxed state. Keep on trying, a little each day, until you can regularly see something. Later on, this skill will develop into a valid form of far-seeing, both in physical distance or through time.

All these divinatory arts need much serious study and practice, and it is no use giving up a technique just because you do not get instantly spectacular results. Like all worthwhile abilities you will need to keep on with the basic exercises until you find they suddenly become easy. There are other applications of all these magical arts that you will discover as your expertise progresses, but they also have ordinary benefits. You will find you get useful 'hunches' more often, and that you can sense things about situations or people you would have missed before. You should be able to understand your own life and its ups and downs better, and through this, be of help to those around you. Be patient and ask the God or Goddess to help you see clearly and speak 'sooth'.

8.
THE EQUIPMENT
OF RITUAL

Ritual magic has a great appeal to many people who have
come across some of the most imaginative works of
fiction writers, but in reality it involves dedication, hard
work, patience and attention to detail. Certainly there are
'words of power', great invocations and elaborate settings
of candle-lit altars, exotic regalia and complicated
ceremonial which vary from lodge to lodge, or group to
group, and even from individual to individual. Some of
these rituals are concerned with magical work, like
uncovering new information, creating talismans for
various purposes, or healing; others are concerned with
celebrating certain seasonal festivals or ritual occasions.
Depending on which system the rites are based on, some
ceremonies will involve initiation or the recognition of
magical advancement to a higher degree; or they might
be more pagan in nature, the rituals of witches following
the Old Religion with all its feasts and moon-orientated
gatherings. Some rites are communions, like the Christian
Mass, but older by many centuries, in which all participants join in sharing wine and special bread or cakes.

If you are working alone, some of these major ceremonial occasions may be beyond you until you find the right sort of group to join; but many of them can be quite successfully worked by an individual or a small group of novices. No matter how basic your level of magical working is, ritual must always be undertaken with a conscious purpose and with regard to common sense. Often, in books based on the magical grammars or 'grimoires' of the middle ages, all sorts of weird and wonderful things are suggested. Sacrifices of animals or strange substances are written about, but quite often these are nothing more than a kind of code. Many of the supposed 'animal sacrifices' are in fact common names for herbs, and the resulting substance was actually an incense. Many medicinal plants were called after animals – dog's mercury, horehound, cat's paw, foxtail grass, colt's foot, harebells and so on. There is no valid modern ritual that requires blood, the death of any creature or the harming of any person. If you read that these sort of things are necessary, discard that book, for it is either very out of date, or written by someone who is not a trained magician or occultist.

For every ritual, these things must be considered: What is it for? Where and when can it be done? What equipment, regalia, symbols and other material (such as appropriate incenses, candles and so on) will be needed? How many people are necessary/available to do it?

You will need to begin fairly simply and then build up more and more complicated ritual patterns, to what ever level of complexity appeals to you and your companions. If you are all novices you must go slowly because it can be very strange when things begin to happen in accordance with your ritual purpose. You will need to understand that a ritual is like a telephone number: if you get the codes right and dial it properly, you will get through to the individual, or in this case to the 'power' or angelic force or god/goddess you have called upon. Of course, they can still be out, or the line can be engaged and so you do not get through. In a magical rite, just as in making a telephone call, you will know when the line is engaged or the call unanswered, for there is a definite feeling.

Correspondences

To work ritual you will be using a pattern of colours, numbers, metals, incenses, instruments and so on called 'correspondences'. Magical correspondences are the equivalent of the telephone codes; you will need all of them to get the message through to where you wish it to go. You will have to build up lists of correspondence and gradually acquire the various items which these tell you are relevant to your purpose. For example, if you wish to work for a new job, the correspondences you would need are those of Jupiter. This planet is named after the god concerned with material growth. His colour is usually royal blue and his number is 4. His day is Thursday (Thor's Day, the same god/power in the Norse pantheon). The metal of Jupiter is tin, or sometimes brass, which is a mixture of tin and copper. From this information it might be clear to you that you could make a square (four-sided) blue talisman on a Thursday, call upon Jupiter to answer your plea, and light four royal blue candles, set in tin or brass holders. Alternatively, you and three others, on Thursday, dressed in royal blue and holding wands made of tin, could walk four times round a square altar on which is an incense burner filled with cedar, a talisman of tin painted with the sigil of Jupiter in blue, and invoke for a new job.

For any kind of magical activity you will need a room large enough to set up a small table for an altar, either at the eastern side (or one side which for magical purposes becomes the east) or better still, in the centre. Ideally, you should have a large, square room with several cupboards, but it is possible to manage in a bed-sitter with a suitcase or small box, which contains all your magical gear and can be used as an altar when necessary. Magical robes, equipment and ritual books should always be kept under lock and key as power is built up in and around them and this becomes dissipated if things are just left about. You will save money if you make as much of your equipment as you can; it will also be magically much more powerful. An object bought from a shop is in no way linked with you, but a pot lovingly, even if badly, made by your own hand is a clear link between you and your magic. Much of the traditional equipment of magic is very old and might seem out of date on the verge of the Aquarian Age, but its symbolism is very powerful. Magic does not discard something unless it is found to be useless and the traditional items of wear, the four instruments and elements of earth, water, fire and air still have their parts to play.

Basic Preparation for Ritual

Having tried successfully some meditation, visualisation and perhaps divination exercises, you will first need something to wear. The most comfortable, practical and traditional garment is a floor-length robe, sometimes with a hood, or else worn with a hooded cloak. If you wish to make your own robe, which is really best of all, you can do so quite simply, for modern fabrics offer a wide range of colours, textures and weights.

First of all you must measure your height from the floor to the top of your shoulder. You will need a piece of material twice this length by about 48 inches, or 1.2 metres, wide. Choose dark blue, brown, green or black as a basic colour to begin with, and look at fabrics which are easy to wash and drip dry.

You can buy a shop pattern for a kaftan or dressing gown if you wish to make an elaborate robe, or you can buy something of this nature; but a magical robe is easy to make to the following pattern and requires very little sewing (experts can add details and embroidery to the basic shape). You will need the measurement from your shoulder to the ground, and your chest/bust measurement. Fold your piece of material in half so that it is exactly your height (A in Figure 1) and cut off any extra. Fold the double material in half longways so you have a strip half the material wide by your height. At the centre cut a quarter circle C (Figure 2) to make neck hole, with a short slit on front side. At the edge measure 14 inches from top fold and place a pin there. Add 10 inches to your chest

measurement and divide by four. Twelve inches down
from the fold place a pin; from there go in this distance.
That gives you the position of the armpit of the robe. Cut
from the pin in the edge to this pin in a sloping line, then
cut down to the bottom so that the hem is about 36-40
inches on each half. When you are sure you have sorted
this out unfold the piece of cloth, which ought now to
look like the letter T. Turn it wrong side out and sew from
cuff to armpit to hem. Neaten the neck opening, perhaps
insert a pocket into the side seam (invaluable for ritual
handkerchief or a box of matches!). If the sleeves are not
quite long enough, add a strip from the spare material.
You can cover the join with a length of braid, which can
also be used around the neck or hem if you wish. The
seams can be sewn by hand or machine. Before turning up
a hem, do try the robe on for length. You may need help
to get it just right, but it can be done in an evening, even
by a complete novice. (Needlework is another skill you
have gained!)

The other very simple thing to make is a cloak, and if
you really cannot manage the robe, then this is a necessity.
Get a wide piece of fabric with a length from your heels to
your shoulders and either turn over a hem or thread a
ribbon in and out to gather up the top edge. You will need
the ends of the gathering ribbon to tie it on with. You
ought to try to make a hood, too, as this helps keep you
warm and cuts out distracting objects from the sides of
your eyes.

As well as the robe you will need a cord or belt to go
round your waist, some soft slippers or sandals for your
feet, and possibly a hat, biretta, nemyss or coronet,
according to taste. Refer to books of historical stage
costumes to discover something appropriate. A simple
headband may be made of strands of silver or gold elastic,
available at Christmas time, plaited loosely and joined
into a circle. This circlet will always fit, and will keep long
hair out of your eyes and away from the hot incense
burner! See what you can design. The waist cord may be
any colour, and it is quite an inexpensive way of having
something of the correct colour for a specific planetary

DESIGN FOR A TRADITIONAL MAGICAL ROBE

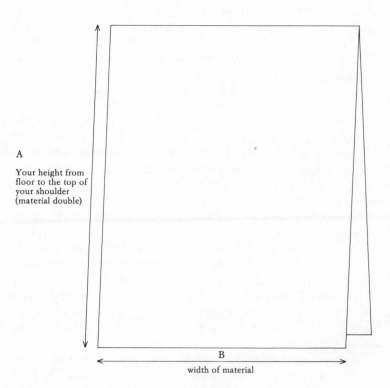

A

Your height from
floor to the top of
your shoulder
(material double)

B

width of material

Figure 1.

C

Cut circle and hem
to fit your neck.
(Leave slit at front
to get your head
through!)

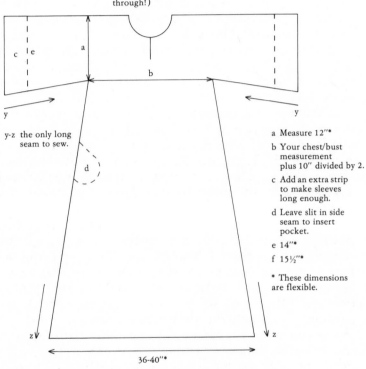

y-z the only long
seam to sew.

a Measure 12″*

b Your chest/bust
measurement
plus 10″ divided by 2.

c Add an extra strip
to make sleeves
long enough.

d Leave slit in side
seam to insert
pocket.

e 14″*

f 15½″*

* These dimensions
are flexible.

Figure 2.

ritual. You can buy plain silk cord or dressing gown belts with tassels in many colours, and often market stalls sell coloured braids, sew-on patches and embroidery silks.

As you progress with your practical work you will probably find you need other items of wear for special ceremonies, or if you become a member of a lodge you may be expected to devise different coloured items for particular ceremonies. These can be cloaks, made of brightly coloured cloth, or sashes, or tabards (made out of a strip of material the width of your shoulders and usually about knee length, often with heavy fringes to make it hang well) or an over-robe, which may be sleeveless.

If you wish to celebrate rituals in public places, or out of doors, or if you like to work naked, there is one very simple piece of regalia you could find useful. This is a ritual ribbon. Take about 2 yards (or 2 metres) of wide ribbon, fold it in half and across the fold, sew a seam at 45 degrees. Cut off the excess triangle of material. This makes a point which hangs down your back and may have a tassel if you wish. The ends may be turned up to form pockets into which a book of words, talismans, or ritual objects may be placed. The ribbon can be embroidered, have applique designs or even painted symbols on it. Ritual ribbons are cheap to make from offcuts of ribbon, or cloth, they can be carried about in a pocket or handbag, so that you always have your magical robe about you, and they can be any colour or material to suit the purpose of every ritual. They can be offered at initiation or to mark the gaining of specific grades and so on.

Once you have made a robe or similar item of ritual clothing it should be kept aside and not worn to fancy dress parties or just to show off. You will find that any object used for ritual purposes will build up an atmosphere about itself, and this should be preserved by keeping all magical materials in a closed cupboard, box or suitcase, well out of the way of the curious. At a later stage you will probably be able to dispense with some regalia or ritual instruments, but while still a novice these 'props' are very valuable.

The Four Elements

Traditionally, a magician has a wand, a pentacle, a cup and a sword. If you have studied the Tarot you will have come across these symbols already and some of their correspondences. Today, although a fully set-up ritual magician will have these instruments, they have to be made, acquired or altered to suit a special purpose. For a novice, simpler alternatives are possible. The basis of Western magic, whichever system you may choose to follow, is that of the four elements. Earth, Water, Fire and Air are each symbolized by something on the altar, which may be shared during a communion ceremony, or by an instrument, or by some item which is magically seen to represent each element. By meditating on each element in turn and choosing something which seems to you to be representative, you can build up sets of items to use. Obviously, you can go for the Pentacle of Earth, the Cup of Water, the Sword of Fire and the Wand of Air if you have access to such traditional symbols, or you can find other things that seem more appropriate to you. Usually there are the four weapons and four items on the altar which are also symbolic of the elements. These may be a rock or stone, some bread or salt for Earth, a dish or shell containing water or a cup of wine for Water, a candle or lantern for Fire and an incense burner or joss sticks or a scented flower or even a fan to represent Air.

The four elements are very important because they form the key that links the inner workings of magic with the outer ones. When you begin to examine your character, perhaps with the aid of your horoscope, you will find that you had certain planets in the signs ruled by the different elements. Earth signs are Taurus, Virgo and Capricorn; Water rules Cancer, Pisces and Scorpio, Fire is Aries, Leo and Sagittarius, and the Air signs are Gemini, Libra and Aquarius, Each makes a kind of filter, like colour filters in photography, so that it colours the effect that the planets have upon the individual character. You will probably have come to see that you have an earthy nature, a watery or emotional side, a fiery temper or an airy-fairy imagination. By working with the symbol you choose to use in ritual magic you will strengthen any aspects of your character which seem weak in that respect.

Obviously you will have to work within your own circumstances, but buying expensive equipment is no substitute for putting effort into making things yourself, even badly, for use in magic. If you are hard up you will have to adapt things you already have, or hunt for bargains. The most important thing is a table or the top of a bookcase, a chest of drawers or a large box which serves as your altar. This may have religious connotations, but it is really a work bench. It will need a cover, perhaps a white table cloth, or a black square of material on which different coloured cloths or paper can be placed to harmonize with your ritual purpose. Make sure that the basic cloth is clean and pleasant to look at and that everything is kept away from lighted candles. Incidentally, you will need at least five candle holders. These can be made out of lumps of modelling clay, or from crack-filling plaster, moulded in a yogurt pot. It is best to use the mould upside-down so that they are wider at the base and less likely to fall over. Simple candle holders can often be bought around Christmas from chain stores, but whatever type you decide on, make sure they will take a tall candle without falling over easily. Although various coloured candles may be required for specific rituals it is better to buy a stock of ordinary white household candles, as these are fairly cheap, will give a good light and can be dipped in melted colouring crayon to give them a coat of whatever colour is required. To make a lantern for the centre of the altar you can take a small jar, dip the bottom of a candle in petroleum jelly, support this in the centre of the base with strips of card, and then fill the jar with about an inch of small pebbles and then fairly runny plaster. Let this set firm over night and lift out the candle. You should have a safe lantern in which short pieces of candle can be safely burned. This design can also be used for candle-holders intended for outdoor use.

You need five lights because traditionally you always have one in the centre of the altar to represent the Light of the Universe, or the spark of God at the centre of your working, and one candle at each point of the compass. If you are not able to actually place one light at each quarter, don't worry; but you will probably need at least five or six candles for specific sorts of rituals. Use your imagination to design safe and pleasant looking items, even if they cost very little. An hour of work and effort put into making the equipment you need will pay dividends, for the power of the object is much greater than a new, bought object. Do not be afraid to experiment.

You will need to find containers for water, salt, oil and incense because in order to consecrate and make everything you use magically powerful, these things will be needed. Small dishes, tiny jamjars or other glass pots are well worth keeping for storing consecrated materials, incenses, herbs and so on. You will begin to examine many things you have about the house to see if they can be adapted for magical use, and searches round second-hand shops may turn up useful items. Whatever you do choose (even natural objects, like stones, seashells, flowers, pieces of wood) will need to be consecrated before they are used in magical work. Consecration 'washes away' any unpleasant connections an object might have; without this, the atmosphere of a ritual can be disturbed.

Incense
Most rituals require incense and as this is something you might not have had to deal with before, here are a few hints. Although joss sticks can be used, the gums and resins associated with the planets and powers in Western magic are not usually made into joss sticks. Joss sticks produce pleasant scents, but they do not give the clear smoke nor the subtle 'psychic' atmosphere which is so important in ritual work. You will find it is worth the trouble to get some real incense, which comes in the form of grains in various brownish shades. It is necessary to get some blocks of charcoal, usually containing a little nitre which makes them light quickly (these are available from specialized equipment stockists: see page 00). Barbecue

charcoal can be used, but it may be difficult to light and it does not burn steadily. Incenses can be bought as blends, such as 'Basilica' or 'Glastonbury', from church suppliers, or as pure gums and resins which you mix yourself. Again, the specialist suppliers will help you. Some make planetary incenses, or ones suitable for particular gods or festivals.

To burn incense you will need either a proper thurible on chains, or a heat-proof ceramic dish. You can use a fireproof bowl part filled with clean sand, but you must be careful as incense gets very hot indeed and can take the varnish off a table if the burner is not insulated. If you intend to carry the burner about during a ritual, to cense the room or make magical gestures with, make sure the container cannot fall over and burn you. A small metal tray or baking tin can be used. For standing an incense burner on the altar, a tile or section of roof slate or wood, painted dull black, can be used to prevent scorching the altar cloth. This is particularly important if you are using a paper cover to accord with the correspondences for a particular power. Ideally, a sheet of plate glass can be used to cover anything inflammable.

Holy oil is occasionally needed, and though this can be bought from specialist suppliers, it is possible to buy a small bottle of almond or olive oil from a chemist and decant a little into another bottle, to which chips of cedar, pine or ground resin can be added to scent the oil. This is used to consecrate metal or pottery.

If there are several of you trying to work magic together you will be able to share the work of finding, making or adapting all the equipment you will require. Some items can be used by anyone, but each of you should have your own robe, cloak or tabard and other regalia, and each of you should have a pentacle, a cup and a wand. If you use a sword in ritual, this can belong to the group, although, of course, if each person achieves one of his or her own, it can be used when necessary. A small, sharp knife each is useful.

The Pentacle and Chalice
The pentacle is an Earth symbol so should be made of

wood, clay, slate, or stone. It is a magical shield; it is the floor upon which you stand and the top of your altar, although in practical terms pentacles are usually made about six to twelve inches across. You must design the pattern upon it yourself, because it symbolizes your own position on the Earth, and no one can tell you what that is. It may be carved, painted, decorated with other materials, engraved or etched, depending on your skill. During your original meditations you should have discovered something about yourself and the Earth and the Universe, so by looking at your magical diary, you may get valuable clues which will help with the design. Even if you cannot paint or draw, it is better to make the pentacle yourself, imaging as you do so the link that you have with the Earth, with Mother Nature, or God the Creator.

The next item is the magical cup or chalice. This should be a gift, given in love, not something simply bought to use. It symbolizes the emotional part of you which, like the cup, controls the shape of the liquid within, and directs your feelings and imagination. If no one cares for you enough to give you this unsought gift, then you will need to work on the emotional part of yourself. Try loving those about you, sending out good thoughts rather than acting selfishly. Give and you *WILL* receive. Suddenly you will discover a coffee mug turns up for your birthday, or perhaps a tea service arrives as a Christmas gift. Once you have received a cup, you can buy or adapt a goblet of glass, a silver chalice or pewter wine cup for ritual use.

The Sword and the Wand

A ritual sword stands for determination and is often used to set a magical seal of protection about the working place. It may be placed to guard the door during a working, or else it lies upon the altar as a symbol of the strength of unity among the members. Although it is a weapon, it should not be thought of as something used to attack others or that cuts away connections, except in very rare circumstances. The traditional ritual sword is about 33 inches long, with a cross shaped hilt. Many of these are now decorative daggers or stage props rather than ancient fighting blades. It is better to use a symbolic sword than a real one, for any traces of battle or fighting can be very hard for a novice to banish completely, and the feeling of fear, pain or combat can linger a ling time and will be picked up during the raised levels of awareness used in magical working. From an occult point of view, a sword bejewelled with fake stones and with a blunt, etched blade is a far safer thing to have about than a real battle weapon, with all its gory history.

The last item of ritual equipment is a wand. This again must be made by the individual and can be painted, carved, or polished natural wood. It ought not to be too long, especially if you are working in a small space. You will have to consider what it represents, having been derived from the arrow or lance of the soldier of old. It flies through the air, carrying with it your intention; in many workings, it is used to seal the lodge and conjure up the guardian spirits. Think hard about what it means to you before launching into a lot of hard work. You can buy a piece of dowelling or cut a stick from a tree. You can carve spirals, or wind it with ribbons. At the ends you can have spheres, lance heads or metal ferrules, carved terminals or painted designs — so long as you understand the symbolism and it makes sense to you.

If you are uncertain about making these pieces of equipment you can meditate upon the four Tarot suit aces, or visualize pictures of the magical work you wish to do, seeing what sort of equipment you would find most useful. As you work on each item, think of how it is an extension of a part of your inner self. The pentacle is your shield of self-sufficiency; the cup your ability to feel and sympathize; your sword or knife is the part of you that can make a way clear ahead and get round obstacles; the wand is your purpose, your will to succeed and the application of your inner strength. Even if collecting, making and perfecting this equipment seems a laborious process, it is time well spent, for like any other exercise intended to build up your physical muscles, gradual work brings greater strength and longer powers of endurance.

When you have made everything, find a safe place to

keep it all. A robe and other regalia, and the four elemental weapons, and the objects to contain the elements on the altar, the candle holders and so on will need a special place. These things are not toys and should always be treated with respect and care, and kept clean and ready for use. Once they have been consecrated and dedicated to a magical purpose they will take on a life of their own.

While you are making these pieces of occult hardware you can be working on building up tables of correspondences for each. Divide a page in your magical notebook vertically into five columns. Across the tops of columns one to four write the names of the instruments — Pentacle, Cup, Sword and Wand. In the fifth column write 'Instrument' and underneath that write 'Element', 'Colour', 'Point of the Compass' and so on down the fifth column. Then fill in the relevant information.

9.
THE RITE WAY
TO WORK

Ritual magic is usually thought of as the art of commanding spirits to obey your will, or changing base metal into gold by using strange 'words of power'. Fiction writers describe nameless rituals held in deserted ruined abbeys, where anyone coming across the magical work is immediately struck dumb or mad or both. In reality, ritual is the highest form of use of a trained imagination and will. It requires skill, patience and a great deal of hard work. It may produce instant results but these will be the culmination of a long hard slog, gaining the basic knowledge, collecting the correct equipment, discovering the appropriate astrological moment, and so on.

Magic can only be safely and effectively worked if you are fully in control of your own self. It is no good, frivolously trying a rite from some ancient book of magic. The results are likely to be very frightening, uncontrolled and long-lasting. It is like driving a racing car in a Grand Prix race the day after passing your driving test. You may have heard of black and white magic; in fact there is no such thing as black or white magic only black or white magicians: If you set out to work magic for selfish reasons, using cruel or ancient methods, that is black magic. If you work for the benefit of others, using your knowledge and skills wisely, trying to make the world a better place, albeit in a small way, that is white magic. For selfishness, you will pay dearly in the karmic balance, throughout this life, and several to come.

On the other hand, a student who acts sensibly and learns the different ways to make use of the skills he is gaining will gradually discover just what he is able to do. Although magic is normally applied as a last resort, when all the 'ordinary' things have been tried, it can be used in mundane situations just as effectively as in the specifically occult setting. You can use magical divination to track down a new magical instrument, or find your lost dog. Once you have mastered the basic techniques, you will find uses for them in every area of your life.

Treat magic and the knowledge of its methods with discretion. Even in this day and age anyone who admits to being a magician or a witch is likely to be laughed at, at the very least. There are still people who think anything connected with the occult is evil and harmful. If you study magic seriously it will be part of your undertaking to see that this mis-information is put right, not by bragging, but by explanation. Many things that people do not understand are seen as dangerous, destructive or just plain nasty. Magic is none of these, but because it is not easy to explain the philosophy behind it or the way it works, it remains hidden and therefore distrusted by many people. The occult schools taught discretion and silence for these very reasons, and if you become actively involved you should keep very quiet about your doings. Do not show off your regalia at parties, nor display your magical instruments to curious friends. If you do, these will become magically useless.

The Ritual of Consecration
The act of consecration is one in which a person, garment or piece of equipment casts off its ties with ordinary life and becomes cleansed, blessed and sacred. Most religions

have a form of self-blessing, the most obvious being the way a Catholic will cross himself in a holy place or during mass. The cross is a very ancient, pre-Christian symbol and a similar gesture is used by magicians, and by students of the Qabalah in particular. What you are doing by making this gesture is to set an invisible seal about yourself, which can be seen by the powers with which magicians work and by clairvoyant people as a circle of bluish-white light. This helps raise the magician's level of consciousness by sealing him off from the ordinary world and its distractions. Usually there are a set of words said silently as you make the gesture, sometimes in English, sometimes in Hebrew, but there is nothing to stop you making up your own words and gestures.

The magical cross is made by touching your forehead with your first and second fingers (the other fingers and the thumb are tucked into your palm) and saying: '*May the Lord of Light be with me*'. You then touch your solar plexus and say: '*And take the Darkness from me*'. Touching your right shoulder you say: '*Be your strength upon me*'. Touch your left shoulder, saying '*and your wisdom guide me*'. You then make a circle, touching forehead, left shoulder, solar plexus and right shoulder and say: '*So may this be.*' '*So mote it be*' (which means the same in Old English) or '*Amen*', which is the same in Hebrew. Think about what you are saying and analyse your feelings afterwards.

Alternatively, you can describe a pentagram, the five pointed star, or a hexagram, with six places to touch and say something; but in both cases it is wise to complete the gesture with a circle. At the end of a meditation or ritual you make the same gesture, but you can 'unwind' the circle if you wish, to brush it away.

Once you and the others with you have sealed yourselves you will need to apply the same treatment to the place in which you intend to work your rituals. (Obviously, before you begin, you will have gathered together all the necessary equipment, robes and so on, and decided the specific purpose of the ritual.)

It is traditional also to seal the working place, be it coven circle, or magical lodge, or private meditation room. The methods used differ, along with the prayers, instruments and participants; but in general, the four elements are used. You will need portable symbols of Earth, Water, Fire and Air, usually represented by a stone, a bowl of water, a lighted candle and a burner of incense. If you are planning a communion you will need a chalice of wine or fruit juice, some bread, cake or biscuit, and usually salt (*not* sea salt). If there is more than one person and sufficient space, the carrying round of the elements can be shared out, preferably one person per element.

The elements are generally presented with Earth first, then Water, Fire and Air. Each is either carried round the room, with an altar in the centre, or offered up and presented to each point of the compass in turn, beginning with North, then West, then South and finally East. If you have room the presented element is placed on the altar in the same quarter. If salt is used to represent Earth, it may be sprinkled about the room and drops of water also. As you carry each element around say something like: *'Power of Earth (Water, Fire, Air), bless this place; cleanse it and make it sacred. In the name of . . . help my (our) work.'* Again, you can make up your own invocations or prayers, calling on assistance from the Unseen to suit your ideas. This is better than slavishly following some old book, especially if it has 'sonorous names' and 'words of power' that you do not understand. You can be far more specific in your every day language than in mispronounced Greek or Enochian. If you do not know the name of a particular deity, make up a title or description to define exactly what sort of assistance you need.

After you have carried round each element, or raised it to each quarter, you can prepare to consecrate items on the altar. In theory you will have blessed each of the elements as you picked them up and carried them round, saying the blessing as you did so, but you can cup your hands over each in turn and ask a special one as you wish. Say: *'Lord of Air* (or *Lady of Earth), bless this thy creature, in thy Holy Name'*. When you are ready to consecrate your pentacle, cup, dagger and wand you will need to bless the elements, and then either sprinkle or pass the object carefully through the smoke or flame of each element in turn. As you do this you say: *'I bless, consecrate and set apart this... in the name of the spirit of Earth (Water, Fire, Air)'.* When it has been blessed, keep it away from prying eyes. Once you have consecrated your four instruments, your robes, regalia and any other equipment, you should be able to feel the difference between a blessed and unblessed thing. There should be a distinct 'feel' to consecrated items.

You can use the same method of consecration for talismans. You will also be able to go on to the next phase of the ritual, which may be a pathworking, a meditation, healing, scrying, divination, or simply a blessing on the work you aim to do in future.

After this , you can go on to the Communion. This is not a desecration of the Christian Mass but a celebration of the magical principles expressed symbolically by the bread, salt and wine, which are ritually shared with all other magicians and occultists. Even if you are alone, you will be sharing the wine and bread symbolically with all others, and it is customary to pour a drop or two of wine and sprinkle a crumb of bread and salt on the earth as a symbol of this mutual sharing.

Choose words which have a meaning for you. If you associate the bread with the Earth Mother, dedicate it to her; if you associate it with the Lord of Harvest, bless it in his name. The same applies to wine or fruit juice or even spring water: see with whom it seems to link you, and then bless the salt. When these are shared, the bread and salt is offered first and the recipient dips a morsel of bread or biscuit into the salt and eats it. You then offer the wine goblet in both hands and it should be taken with both hands, never just one; this signifies unity and friendship, both among those present and the unseen companions on the path. Together you can sprinkle a little more incense, sniff the scented flower and warm your hands over the candle flame, or even pass these round, if there are enough of you, so that all participate in every element.

When the communion is finished the cup should be

emptied by the last to receive it and it should be turned upsidedown on the plate on which the bread and salt were placed. This should afterwards be tipped on the earth to scatter any dregs of wine and crumbs to the creatures of Nature. (It is best to do this after a rite as it brings you right back to earth.)

The next part of the ritual is the Thanksgiving, during which prayers are said for peace in the world, for healing of the sick, for fertility and success of the Earth herself and to the strengthening of the Lord of Life in the world. You can each say one of these in turn, or choose poems, songs or prayers to fit the occasion, or whatever you feel is right. You should then collect the four elements and walk them round in the reverse direction to 'un-wind' the barrier that surrounds the place of ritual, as you do so saying 'Thank you' to the powers that you may not yet sense. There is no hurry but everything should be dealt with neatly and thoroughly. When you have finished, take off your robe and put it away. Wash up the cup and platter and tidy away all your equipment, especially now it has been consecrated, into its box or cupboard. You may feel very strange if you have never done anything like this before and it is a good idea to have a warm drink and some fruit afterwards. You should also immediately write up your journal with all the details of the type of ritual, the people or their 'magical names' and any thing that occurred to you during the meditation or pathworking.

All incense should be allowed to burn out, but if you wish to quench candles these must always be pinched out or snuffed with an old fashioned snuffer. They should not be blown out because, magically, breath is life and even a flame is a living thing.

Practice the actions of handling round the goblet and bread/salt with your companions. Get used to walking about in a long skirt, and learn to move smoothly in it. See how much room you have for extravagant gestures, especially once you start waving your wand and sword about. If you cannot remember or make up the words of the prayers, invocations and blessings, you will need a book to write out your rituals in, remembering it will probably have to be read in candle light.

If you look back through this chapter you will find all the stages of a traditional ritual set out. It is worth making a list of these so that you can gradually collect prayers and invocations which seem apt to you for each part. You and your companions can decide what you wish to do, and who should do what. It is a good idea to circulate all the parts so that different people get the experience of working in each place.

Initiation

Ideally, people should only work ritual once they have been properly accepted and initiated into a coven or ritual lodge. In today's world, however, at the brink of the Aquarian Age, this is not always possible. There are valid training groups, but these are few in number and they cannot between them cope with all the people who seriously wish to participate in magical work. If you are fortunate enough to come across such a group and be accepted by them, you will have many advantages over the lone student or the group of beginners who have to learn from books such as this; but all is not lost. Once you are certain that the path of magic is the one you earnestly wish to pursue, then you will have to set about the process of self-initiation. This is a very serious undertaking and not something to rush into after a month or so of meditation exercises; but if you have been working on these techniques for about a year, you *MAY* be ready to consider the matter.

As this book is written in the manner of a 'Do-it-yourself' manual, it is not a matter of simply providing a list of rituals to perform, prayers to say and actions to make. The Age of Aquarius is the age of the individual, selecting his or her own path from the many offered. It is up to you to see what sort of religious commitment you wish to make, what gods or goddesses or conventional religious deities you wish to call upon for aid and guidance – only you can choose. You must decide if you want to commit yourself to the magical path from now on, or if you are ready to offer healing, divination or guidance to other people as a result of your studies so far.

Magical commitment is no light undertaking. In the old days the magical schools were run like monasteries and once you had taken your final vows you were under the abbot's bidding for the rest of your days. A magical initiation is just as serious and important a step to take today, and the vows you make, even if you are not being taken into a group, are just as binding. They may even be more so, for it seems that those who have followed the paths of magic in one life tend to return to it in subsequent incarnations. This fact is often recognized by wise teachers of the hidden arts, so that even a young novice may be acknowledged as having been a skilled and well-trained magician in a previous life.

If you are determined to follow this difficult and exciting way, which can lead from your own doorstep to heights you cannot yet dream of, you will need to prepare yourself and all the equipment you will require over a period of time. Look forward and see if it is coming up to a New Year, calendar or solar (21 March), your birthday or some ancient festival which seems appropriate for your 're-birth day'. If such a date is a few weeks or months ahead, make that a time to work towards. Otherwise, examine your horoscope, find out which sign is specially good for commencing things – an astrologer will help you with this if you haven't the skill to decide. Give yourself time to prepare, for far too often magic is an art in which 'fools rush in where angels fear to tread'.

Any magical initiation consists of a number of parts that vary from tradition to tradition, but in most cases the circle or lodge is prepared by the group of initiates and then the candidate is brought in by one of them. He may be asked some questions, which he either answers from his own knowledge or they may be answered for him; he may be blindfolded or restrained in some other way. He will be asked if he agrees with the ideals of the group and will probably be expected to swear an oath of secrecy, honour and commitment to the work of the group. Various tools or symbols will be shown and their use explained to him and he will eventually take his place among his fellows. Perhaps some sort of communion will follow and all that is necessary will be explained as the ritual progresses. Details of various sorts of rituals of this nature have been written about widely, so if you wish you can build up your own knowledge before getting directly involved. Often a candidate is given or chooses a new name or motto by which he is known in the circle, and there is often a 'death-and-rebirth' scene enacted during the ceremony; there may also be cleansing or banishing rites, depending on the tradition concerned. Should you be joining an established group, do ask what is likely to happen, what you might be expected to swear to, and anything else you can think of. If the group is a valid one, someone will explain as much as possible without breaking any rules, and you will feel welcomed and wanted. If this is not the case, think very carefully about it before you commit yourself to some unknown fate!

Any oath that threatens unpleasant penalties to anyone who chooses to leave the group later on, or suggests that it is impossible to break away, should be taken with a pinch of salt. No genuine group will bind its members by anything stronger than their desire to continue with it, and should they wish to leave they will only be asked not to talk about what they learned or where. Fiendish oaths and threats make dramatic reading in novels but have little basis in fact. No one can carry them out and so they cannot be binding. If you do promise to be discreet, to hold with honour to what you have been taught and use your skills to benefit others, try to do so. Promises made under threat of being eaten by demons, or being cut into a thousand pieces and scattered all over the globe, should be treated with the scorn they deserve – and the groups which make such threats avoided like the plague! If you do make a reasonable promise to behave and get on with your fellows and don't keep your word, the gods can find plenty of ways of reminding you, without resorting to horrible penalties!

When you feel ready to take such a step as magical self-initiation you will need to decide exactly what you can reasonably do without upsetting the family. A group of people who are all going to undergo a self-initiation at the same time will also have to select a time and place that is convenient to all. This might prove impossible, so that everyone has to do his or her own thing separately – often this is the best course of action. Because it is going to be a 'do-it-yourself' rite you cannot expect the surprises which are normally arranged by any initiating group, but you will probably encounter one or two strange moments if you go about the matter seriously. (You will probably get worse shocks if you set about it without considering the consequences!)

The first part of many initiations, and especially self-initiations, is the vigil. In earlier times a squire who was to be dubbed a knight would spend the night in a chapel, keeping vigil over his sword and armour placed upon the altar. During the hours of darkness he would examine his conscience, understand what he was letting himself in for, and perhaps his friends or teachers would whisper from the dark corners of the church sins or failings he hoped everyone had forgotten. In the morning he would be bathed by other young knights, his hair would be cut short, and he would be dressed in new clothes. His mother would present his sword, spurs and helmet and he would be dubbed by the king or some senior knight. There was then usually a service of blessing. A magical novice should go through a similar process.

Anyone living alone can arrange a proper vigil, ritual, celebration and consecration of him or herself, but if you have a family you will need to consider them also. It might be possible to perform your ceremony at the home of a friend or magical companion. You may not be able to spend all night watching over your collection of regalia and equipment, but you might be able to take a long walk through a wild or lonely place and during that time think seriously about your commitment to the magical way. No matter how you go about it, once you have committed yourself it is for ever. You will also have to choose a magical name: even lone workers need an inner name to call to the gods, and sometimes they will call it back! This can be a thing, a plant, a motto like 'Sister Seeker of

Truth' or 'Brother Bring Hope to the Earth'. Whatever you select, try to live up to it.

If you can spend a whole night meditating, thinking and considering your future course, in or out of doors, in a mundane or sacred place, you will certainly be guided on your path from then on. It is possible to be alone at an ancient sacred site, and novices have stayed in long-barrows, on top of magical hills or alone on a deserted beach — anywhere, in fact, where you can really think what you are doing in peace and quiet. It is possible that you do not really yet understand what such commitment will actually mean, and this is equally true of a novice who is being initiated into a group or coven. A wise leader will ensure that the newcomer is instructed and any queries or doubts ironed out before he gets as far as an initiation rite; but when you are walking this path alone you can only rely on that inner certainty that it is right to proceed, and be patient if you are not sure.

When you are convinced you are making the right move, you will need to make a promise. If you are doing this alone you obviously cannot swear to anyone else, but any promise you make is between you and the God/Goddesses you wish to serve. You cannot ignore this aspect of initiation: if you do not set yourself some sort of limit you may find you have to undertake things which are beyond you. Do not make endless vows to work with a specific person, nor to support only one idea: you are growing in your magical knowledge and what lies ahead may change your direction. Make a serious promise to try to learn as much as you can, to apply your knowledge for the benefit of others rather than selfishly, to honour the beliefs and practices of others, no matter how odd they may seem to you, to act responsibily with any skills you develop. If you have decided which God or Goddesses, power, angelic force or humanitarian view you wish to support, you can make your vow in their name. You may make your promises with your hand upon symbols of Earth, Water, Fire and Air in turn, or just touch bare earth, and swear by the power of the earth and the sky above to be true to whatever you have vowed. Work all this out well in advance.

Many people do not understand the principle of magical commitment or responsibility, but you soon learn it in practice. Whenever you make a magical act you are, as it were, making a move in the chess game of life. If you make a change that is anti-evolutionary, selfish or simply very stupid you will have to settle the karmic debt later on. This is especially important if you insist on using your newly-gained magical abilities to meddle in the lives of other folk.

It might seem a good idea to try to bring together parted lovers or to perform a ritual to make yourself some money; but you will nearly always find that either the ritual goes wrong or that you just cannot do it. The reason is that sometimes people have to learn that their path is a lonely one, or that it is possible to cope with less money than they would like. These situations teach valuable lessons and if you try to avoid them, or make other people avoid similar experiences, they will only have to be faced at some other time. You may be tempted to use your magical skills to interfere with the activities of other people, and you may even be asked to act in various ways to help them. You must be very careful at not becoming involved in these situations because when you start to change the pattern of somebody else's life it will reflect on your own. Think very carefully, especially now, before you commit yourself to the magical way forever. Are you ready to advise, to guide and help those who may come to you, and are you wise enough to say 'No!' from time to time? It is very important to understand that your responsibility will extend to all areas in which you use magical methods.

When you have decided what you are prepared to swear upon, you must draft what you intend to promise — to hold in honour the magical arts, to strive for peace in the world, to try to learn more and so help people more effectively, to grow into the best person you can possibly be, and to build your own contacts with the God and Goddesses, in what ever form you perceive them. Work it all out, and write it down so you can say exactly what you feel to be right. Perhaps there will be no other human to hear your words, but you can be certain that the Guardians of the Mysteries will hear and take note of your promise.

After this you could lay out all your tools and equipment, and, as if you were teaching a novice, go over each item, saying what it is for, how you intend to use it, what it seems to symbolize. You can then have a few moments of meditation to see if all is going on well. Next you might have your communion of bread and salt and a cup of wine. It is traditional to pour a small libation at this time, and if you are indoors a bowl of earth from your garden, or from a sacred place, can be used to represent the Earth upon which you make your offering. Imagine that as you eat the bread dipped in salt that you are sharing with the Great Brotherhood of initiates all over the world. You may well even see them about your room, within the circle. Scatter a few crumbs upon the Earth, sip the wine, pouring a few drops for the Lord of Creation. Again, wait a little while, perhaps savouring your drink and consecrated bread, waiting for a feeling of companionship.

You can now add a little more incense to the charcoal, giving thanks for inspiration and guidance, for warmth of the sun and for friendships. You may have a new piece of regalia which you have not worn, or a cord which you can put on to show that you are binding yourself to the path you have chosen. In fact you can symbolically adopt the dress of the robed orders. The robe symbolizes the perfected you which you are striving to become, the sandals or slippers the path you intend to walk in the Mysteries. The headdress or circlet is your higher, inner self which guards and guides. The girdle, cord or belt binds you to the promise you have made, so that you do not forget what you have sworn. The talisman you may wear about your neck on a ribbon is the symbol of the tradition you wish to follow — the Christian cross, the Egyptian ankh, the witch's pentacle, the equal-armed, circled cross of the oldest magical schools, or any other symbol which is sacred to you.

After you have ceremonially adopted the robes and regalia you have chosen, you should say a prayer to each quarter, one for peace in the world, one for enlightenment and understanding, one for healing the sick, and another blessing the land for its gifts, fertility and the fruits of field and orchard. Work these out for yourself and use them in your own ceremonies of communion or magic.

You may like yet another period of assimilation and meditation before you finally close the circle. When you are ready (and this ritual can have a very profound effect on you, even if you are thoroughly prepared), close the circle by collecting the symbols of the elements and walking them round anti-clockwise to bring the power down to its ordinary level. Place each in turn on the altar, say a formal thank you to all the invisible (or theoretically invisible) deities and powers who have attended your work. These are never dismissed as you do not have the right to command them or order them about. Make sure you feel yourself to be back to normal before finally pinching out any candles and completely unwinding whatever symbols you used to seal the place.

You will probably need a good night's sleep after all this, so avoid a day of wild activity immediately after a self-initiation ritual. The effects on you may be felt during the actual ceremony, immediately afterwards, or even several days or weeks later. Do not expect ten-foot high angels to appear and offer you a crown of gold or a signed charter from God; the feeling will be intensely personal, inward and uplifting. It can be a frightening experience unless you are really ready to take this step, and there is never a reason to rush into any magical activity until you know enough to undertake it safely.

Again, the course of this first ritual is not set out for you to simply copy and perform. You will need to read and re-read this chapter, sorting out the various stages, deciding exactly what you can do and what you want to do, how it can be arranged, when and where. Plan, rehearse and prepare everything well in advance as this will all help to ensure the actual day goes smoothly and nothing is forgotten. If you do miss something out, mime it, or quickly re-think what you are doing. Once you have made your circle, you are committed.

10.
A WEEK OF
MAGICAL WORK

Although there are many applications of magical work you will need to become used to ritual, divination and all the other arts at your own pace before undertaking any ceremonies which may occur to you. One thing you will need to do is to build up a table of correspondences for the seven planets of traditional systems of astrology etc. As each one of these applies to a day of the week, it is worth taking this concept as a starting point. Make another chart with the days of the week across the top and enter under each one the appropriate planet, the metal, the number, the gem, the colour and incense and so on.

Perhaps it is best to begin with Sunday. On the Saturday you can decide what the main purpose of your week's work is to be – this could be the search for a new occupation, some aspect of personal development, a quest for knowledge, mastering a new occult skill or the healing of a sick friend. In general, the stages would be the same, but the symbols and so on would be different, and you might like to use your own symbol of the god/goddess/deity/power which is relevant to the objective. Think everything out and write a list of your requirements, the purpose of the working and any other important information in your magical book.

It is not necessary to go to elaborate lengths to make use of the relevant correspondences, but if you have a robe you can also wear a coloured girdle, or a charm on a ribbon about your neck. Another way to match the colours to the ritual is to have a sheet of plate glass on your altar top and underneath it lay sheets of paper, foil or cloth of the appropriate hue for your purpose; if you are using real candles and hot incense do take precautions against setting fire to something — or someone. Sheets of wrapping paper can often be found in various metallic colours, like silver, gold, scarlet, green, blue, purple, yellow and so on, and these will be very useful for ceremonies associated with a particular planetary purpose. Use your imagination and commonsense when choosing things to wear or display on your altar for any ritual.

Sunday and Monday

Sunday is of course the day of the Sun. It is a day to work for healing as the Sun is the life-bringer and its light is beneficial to anyone who is ill. It is also the 'planet' concerned with the personality, the self and, magically, with the inner light of occult knowledge. Bear all this in your mind as you begin to set up your week's work. You may carry out your Sunday rite during the day, when the actual Sun is above the horizon. The number of the Sun is one: the colour/metal gold. The wand should be almond wood; the incense is galbanum. You can work out how you go about incorporating these into your own working. If you are making a talisman it could be written in gold or yellow on a circular base by the light of one candle and your wear something gold/yellow as you do it; more expensively, a healing talisman could be inscribed on a gold disc, studded with diamonds and perfumed with frankincense.

Monday is the day of the moon and is more concerned with matters of a psychic nature, women (whose lives are to some extent ruled by the moon's phases) and visions.

You will need to work when the moon is above the horizon (which can be during the day). A study of the phase of the moon, her position and rising and setting times is valuable to any magician because she has a powerful effect on any magical enterprise. You may wear white or silver, or even dark purple, and the number of the moon is two, so you will need two candles. A talisman ought to be made of silver and should be a crescent shape. Recognize the difference between a waxing and waning shape as these have different magical significances. The waxing, growing moon is concerned with increase and the outward showing of psychic or inspirational matters; the full moon is the date of pagan celebrations concerned with the Goddess as Mother, and the waning, fading moon takes away things — for instance ill health, bad luck or nightmares. You will need to select the correct phase for the moon to work with you.

The perfume of the moon is jasmine, and as a drink for moon rites you can try jasmine tea, white wine or the juice of white fruits. Gems include moonstones, crystals or white quartz, and often cheap tumble-polished stones can be found to incorporate into any talisman of the moon. Silver foil can be used instead of the metal silver; again, use your imagination as to what is appropriate.

As the moon is concerned with psychism, Monday is a good time for any sort of divination, particularly scrying, or crystal-gazing. This is a skill (see page 83) requiring patience and the ability, gained through meditation and similar exercises, to switch to a different mode of consciousness where physical relaxation combines with mental alertness and psychic perception. The sealing of a circle magically will go a long way to cutting down your perception of disturbing external noises or thoughts. You should bless your crystal or glass ball or dark mirror in the name of the Lady of the Moon in her guise as Goddess of inspiration. You can sprinkle it with blessed water, and any scrying glass or speculum should always be kept wrapped up in a dark cloth — velvet or silk are usual as these keep the magical charge inside and make the exercise easier.

Once you have shifted your level of awareness into an inner mode of perception you will need to concentrate on any images, symbols or pictures that drift into view. This is not easy and takes a while to master, but any form of scrying is a valuable adjunct to magical ability, for it is in this way that you are able to perceive the forces around your circle, and the way in which your spell will come into effect. You will also quickly be certain when your working is going to fail, and you will also realize why. Scrying can take quite a while as you tend to lose awareness of time, and if you get into an informative session you must be prepared to see it through; so do not try to fit your Monday rite into the time before some other activity. Often a short spell of meditation using the moon as a focus will bring surprising insights into the problem or matter on which you are working and it may indicate a direction in which to continue your work that had not previously occurred to you. Be prepared for unexpected hints — even after your set time, because the faculty of inspiration may not work on your ordinary time scale. Do act on any information gained this way, as it is advice from your inner self.

Tuesday and Wednesday

Tuesday is ruled by Mars, the planet usually associated with fighting and soldiers. Mars is also concerned with courage, strength and determination. His number is eight, the colour blood red, the metal iron, and his incense is tobacco. Often Dragon's Blood resin is used in rituals of Mars as it is dark red and has a sharp martial scent. If you are working a week of magic, now is the time to stress your determination and to call upon the God of Strength and Success to aid you win the battle for your aim. It also is the day to bless or consecrate your dagger or sword, whilst wearing something fiery red, on an altar covered with scarlet, and iron or stainless steel dishes for salt and water.

The Tuesday ritual can be tough going because you may come face to face with your own weaknesses, anger and with memories of these times when you lacked the courage of your convictions. You must demonstrate the qualities of Mars in your own nature, preferring the constructive strengths to the cruelty and overbearing nature of the warrior. You should recognize that mercy is a virtue shown by the greatest warriors.

Magic requires courage, for every ritual is an experiment in which you are working with forces far greater than you can imagine. You will be required to show both strength and humility. You will need will power to go through with some activities and, like a sportsman making a bid for a record, you will often have to give every ounce of effort to achieve what you have set your heart upon. Dion Fortune wrote: 'If you have a choice of taking up magic or going into the blacksmithing trade, enter the forge for the work is much lighter!' She was right, for it is foolish to think that magic is easy. You *can* learn to wave a magic wand and achieve what you wish, but it takes as much effort on your part as climbing a great mountain or gaining a University degree. Meditate on all aspects of courage and skill, valour and determination. Strangely, this can apply just as much to female magicians as to male, for they may have children to defend, homes to manage alone, and careers in areas usually considered to be male provinces. There have been a number of fully trained priestesses who wield their magical swords with as much right and power as any male adept, for the mage is one who balances the male and female parts equally, and can function in either magical role.

Wednesday is the day of Mercury (*Mercredi* in French, or Woden's day in Saxon). He is the messenger of the gods, the communicator and bringer of news, a great traveller, but also a joker and thief, so beware of this aspect of the Mercurial nature. His colour is either orange, according to Qabalistic symbolism, or light blue; his metal is quicksilver or mercury, but today talismans for travel are made of aluminium. His number is five, and his incense is storax.

On Wednesdays you could make travel plans, design talismans for safety or use in all forms of communication, preferably on the mundane rather than the psychic level. If you are working for some material gain it is the time to write letters, make telephone calls and direct your attention to any form of communication that will help with your project. Mercury has a joking aspect, so beware of being misled by a red herring, or have some gain stolen from you by a rival or a misunderstanding. Be certain you know what you are after and exactly what you are doing to achieve it, for misinformation can trip you up now. Mercury's stone is the mystic opal.

Certainly you can meditate and apply your inner senses to discovering new information, but this is a practical day, too. Often news can be received showing that you are on the right lines, or that you have missed a trick somewhere. Be open to change and keep a flexible attitude to anything you learn. Magic *does* work, but the specific manner in which it does so is not easy to predict — even adepts get caught on the hop sometimes! Things can be helped to change and become favourable for you, but do not expect to be able to predict every stage of the transformation. Change is in the hands of the gods, who do not work with either human logic or human restrictions.

Thursday and Friday

Thursday is a time to make use of your knowledge about Jupiter, whose power is that of expansion and growth, especially in the field of material success, business acumen and luck. You may find that you actually get somewhere on a Thursday if you wish to progress in material matters. Jupiter's colour is a rich royal blue; his number is four, so you could make square talismans from his metal, which is tin. Often brass is used, as tin is now a rare metal. The incense of Jupiter is cedar. This wood is used for cigar boxes as well as garden sheds and it may be possible to get small pieces that can be shaved into tiny splinters to burn on charcoal, though like all the other gums and resins, cedar can be bought from a specialist supplier.

Rites to Jupiter require the most sumptuous setting, with rich robes and fine candles in deep blue, or even royal purple. His gem is amethyst and a talisman for success could be made of tin or brass with four of these jewels set in a square; alternatively, it could be cut from royal blue paper and the sacred names written in gold as a contrast. You will find you receive meditational guidance about material activities during a Jupiter rite and might even feel impelled to make investments to help your money grow, or plant seeds of some sort for the future.

You have the chance to examine your own position in the world and see how you can expand your own empire. Through your magical skills you will be able to take a helpful role, giving wise guidance and inspired instruction to people who may come to you for help. It may well surprise you how your abilities, which seem mystical and other-worldly, have practical, down-to-earth applications in your ordinary life. Any healing skill, especially if you have had the sense to study conventional first aid or emergency treatment in cases of illness or accident, can come into play in the street, at work and in the home. You will find the self-assurance that develops in the wake of magical skill will carry you through difficult or dangerous times, and your calmness, knowledge and practical abilities can often turn an emergency into a safe situation. Jupiterian magic can often be applied in this way, just as it can in the running and reorganizing of any business activity. As you become adept at various magical activities you will find that your 'empire' or circle of influence will spread and more opportunities for you to succeed will arise.

Friday brings the day of Venus, the Goddess of Love. Her colour is green, her metal copper, her stone emerald or green agate, her active principle is love, harmony, partnership and her number is six. Many people imagine that magic can be effectively used in affairs of the heart, and in some respects they are right; but magic gives no one the authority to interfere in any way in the lives of others. Imagine you were on the receiving end — would you like having your affairs manipulated and your relationships dictated by someone else? If you wish to use magic to gain the love of someone else you will find your spells work — but on you. You will become someone lovable, your attitudes will change so that you actually attract the sort of company you seek; but you cannot change other people to suit your wants.

Often people ask for talismans for love without realizing what will happen if they try to impel the affections of another person. They end up burdened for years, perhaps, or even several lives, with an unwilling, unhappy and joyless partnership, united not by love but by knots of karmic debt that can take ages to unravel. To win love you must give it out; you must be someone whom people long to be with. Then you will get as much love as you give out.

You can certainly use the attributes of Venus to help you in your work. She is concerned with all kinds of partnerships, harmonies and feelings of unity, which can apply to many situations of ordinary life. She teaches inner harmony as well as outer balance, victory over the less well controlled parts of human nature, gentleness, patience and co-operation with all levels of our beings. She is also Mother Nature and anything to do with the natural world can be worked under her symbols and power. She is strong, for it is written that 'Love makes the world go round'. It is also well known that love will overcome all sorts of odds, not only in fairy tales like Beauty and the Beast and Sleeping Beauty, but in everyday events. Many acts of courage or heroism are due to love of life rather than to some idea of material reward. It is seen in the way people react in a crisis, performing great feats of strength, daring and courage, not because of a war or struggle, but to rescue a trapped kitten! That is the effect of Venus, overcoming natural fears of fire or water, and her strength is greater than that even of Mars, for it is unselfish.

If you lack inner harmony, put on a green robe or cord, find some item of copper, six green candles and a rose or benzoin incense and see what a meditation on Venus will do for you. Green used to be thought of as an unlucky colour because it was associated with the fairies; but as green is a magical colour it can be safely worn by anyone who recognizes its importance. Try to work with and for others, not for selfish ends, and the Goddess of Life and Harmony and Love will bless you and her power will guide you in the darkest times.

Saturday

On Saturday you come to the end of a week of effort with the planet Saturn. He is the old man of the universe; his power is constrictive, limiting, his colour black, his metal lead and his jewels jet and onyx. He is a hard task-master, ruling with a firm hand, fencing us in to a world of tough reality. He sets edges to any enterprise, but as we grow older we come to a greater understanding of his basic wisdom and stillness. In old age we are his companions and can work within the boundaries he makes for us without wasting energy. His rituals are slow and solemn, conducted in sonorous tones. His incense is the bitter myrrh, the perfume of sacrifice and self-abasement. In a week of magic it is the time to consolidate all that has been gained, reflect upon advances made and set limitations on new ventures. He is also stability and can make a firm foundation for any future activity, and his strong fence can keep out unwanted distractions and influences.

Saturn rules the ends of life and light, yet he is not a cruel tyrant but a firm grandfather who can see his children's mistakes and tries to guide them on a sensible path, usually to be rewarded by being called a silly old fool. In his age is wisdom and common sense, yet it is hidden in the dark cloak of experience and suffering, which makes it hard for the young and inexperienced to talk the same language. His stern solid nature is easy to dismiss in a hasty life, yet when things start to disintegrate around us, or when our castles in the air are discovered to lack the foundations of reality, it is to the Saturnian powers we must turn for support.

Some talismans made of lead contain a Roman acrostic, a Latin invocation which is sometimes used as a good luck charm. There are many interpretations of SATOR AREPO TENET OPERA ROTAS, but it is certainly a Saturn spell. One translation gives it as 'May the destroying might of the Triple Goddess work until the world has turned full circle.' Not a happy charm! The Triple Goddess has a dark side, sometimes called Hecate or the Morrigan, who has a destructive and dark appearance in her dealings with mankind. She is the Third Fate who cuts the thread of life, spun and measured by her sisters; she, like Saturn, is a limiter and shares the symbolism of the yew tree, the dark of the moon and black stones, which in her case are used for scrying and receiving wisdom. But then youth is not the time of wisdom and understanding, of experience and knowledge; it is the time for action not thought, for outgoingness not reflection, and so the dark ones, Hecate and Saturn, are feared: their stability is seen as a hinderance to living, and their calmness and experience as a fence or barrier to what is so important to youth. They will be more important later, for they are the Masters of Time. They will allow youth its moment, for in old age all of us come into their sphere of influence, whether we like it or not; they can then be seen as friends and strong companions, firm supporters and wise counsellors.

Saturn completes the revolution of a week's magical acts, yet you will see that you can continue, starting a new cycle of healing solar work. Probably you will seldom complete a whole week on any given project, but it is one of the best ways to learn the arts of ritual, the arrangement of symbols, the use of colours, numbers and other correspondences that are given here. Go through this chapter several times, building up a list of the correspondences that are given here for each day, and as you read other books on magic you will be able to gather material on all manner of things relating to each of these planets or days. Later you can add the information for Uranus, Neptune and Pluto, the outer planets that were discovered much more recently. All have a magical application, all are important in the horoscope of any individual and there are a great number of different things attributed to each. In some cases you will find different correspondences given, and it will be up to you to choose which colour or number, etc., seems most appropriate to each planet.

When you have consecrated all your equipment, which you may well continue to add to as time goes on, you will be able to make a talisman for most of the planetary matters, or to help in all sorts of enterprises. You will learn to keep silent about your activities, and not to boast of your successes, nor complain about your failures.

Secrecy adds a great deal of power to magical work, and though it is vital to be completely open and honest with any companions in the work, it is equally important not to brag about your magical interests. If you do show off, turning up to fancy dress parties in your robes, or making charms for people to affect others, or dabbling in the affairs of those who have not asked for help, you will soon wind up reaping the whirlwind you have sown. If you have any psychic abilities, but have not learned the skill of 'switching them off', you will be prey to all manner of unpleasant experiences, all gleaned from unexplored aspects of your own nature — nothing from outside will 'come and get you': it is all there within you already. Being haunted by your own inner fears, failing at the simplest counter magic, losing the power to help, the ability to meditate or be calm is sufficient to show how you have transgressed the code of magical ethics!

There are no vengeful gods lurking unseen, but there are inner depths within you which can be challenged and unravelled, or which can make their presence known, like a rotting carcase, under your nose. If you have seriously tried to get to grips with the factors that make up your human character, and have striven to raise yourself up, nothing can or will harm you. There are no fears you cannot master or overcome by yourself so long as you are really trying to learn and are acting in a reasonable manner. Certainly it will feel very strange the first few times you dress up and perform your rituals. You may feel embarassed and self-conscious, even if you are alone, and doubly so if you have a companion — who is just as likely to feel the same! You will have to get used to moving about in a long skirt in a confined space and of dealing effectively with all the regalia of ritual; you will need to learn to cope with a strange state of consciousness, yet move and walk, talk and think whilst partly in this world and partly out of it.

You will never cease to learn; you will never come to the end of the applications of your magical skills. Each book you read will open new doors, raise questions which can only be resolved by personal discovery. You will have many strange experiences, and with perseverance you will reach new heights of skill and competence. The only limit on what you can achieve is what you set out to do.

11.
THE MANY PATHS
OF MAGIC

If you have worked your way through this book or have already learned many of the techniques described here, you may well be wondering how you can apply the knowledge. From the previous chapter you will see what sort of magic can be successfully worked on each day, and there is enough information to set up a ritual for any purpose, to scry or magically meditate, to make a talisman or work for some other objective. Although there are many sorts of rituals they all follow a similar basic pattern, and though the purpose may be different and the gods and goddesses invoked may vary, or the powers called upon in another way, most rituals are based on the same plan.

To begin with, you will always have to know in advance the aim of the ritual you are about to perform, and though it is possible for some new direction to emerge during the course of the rite, that is another matter. If you are working with others, make sure they know as well, and are in agreement. Write down the purpose in your magical diary, sort out any special regalia, wine, cakes, candles, materials for talismans, scrying balls, or a link with a sick person if it is for healing.

Once you have double checked that everything is ready, and have had a ritual bath or shower, or at least a good wash before any major ritual, put on your robes and sandals slowly. Now is the time to gently shift into your raised magical personality. Say a prayer or a remembrance of the symbolism of the various things you are putting on, recall your magical name or motto — think about this too. Do not rush; it is time to change yourself into the magus you are aiming to become, competent, calm and powerful — this takes a few moments. Go sedately into your magical room or temple, take your place and look around to assure yourself that everything is ready, and that your companions are where you expect them to be, looking calm and alert, awake and attentive. Using which ever form of self-blessing you prefer, make your first ritual gestures, sealing yourselves, lifting your consciousness to a higher, more concentrated level of magical reality.

Now you must use the elements of Earth, Water, Fire and Air to bless the place or circle. Light the central candle or lamp, and then with a taper or spill, light the charcoal for the incense. This will usually take a moment to burn through and stop sparking. Take a small spoonful of incense grains and sprinkle these gently on the hot charcoal — a pinch is enough to begin with. In turn, carry the elements around, pronouncing a blessing and consecration on each in turn, asking for protection and enlightenment. In some lodges the images of the four archangels, Uriel, Gabriel, Michael and Raphael, or the powers of the elements in some other form, are called up to watch over the working, with appropriate prayers. Once this has been done and you and your companions are back in your places, you will continue to the next phase.

Having consecrated and sealed the place, you then have to change it to the magical temple, sacred grove or holy place in which your work is set. This may be a form of pathworking, or a piece of description, a single image or even some music which fits the intention and place which is your setting. This again should be a slow transition as it allows images and feelings to build up and it can have rather strange effects if you rush on too fast, leaving some of your companions behind. St Ignatius Loyola called this 'composition of place' and he taught his monks to recreate in their chapels scenes from the life of Jesus so completely that they became first-hand witnesses to it.

Now is the time to state the purpose of the ritual out loud and to call upon whichever gods/goddesses, powers, angels or other influences are to assist in the work. If you are making a talisman, each stage may need to be blessed, and at the end the completed object will have to be consecrated with Earth, Water, Fire and Air, as described previously. A blessed talisman must be wrapped in a soft cloth (silk is best) to keep its magical charge inside when it is carried around.

You may now like to have a divination session, or a meditation to assess how things are going or receive instructions from the powers with which you are working. This also gives you a chance to remember anything you have forgotten about the work you have done and allows the level of concentration to rise or fall so that you are ready to proceed.

The next phase is the communion or sharing of the magical food and drink. You can use all kinds of things, even have a real feast with several courses, if you wish; but for formal ritual, a shared goblet of red wine and a morsel of bread dipped in salt is sufficient. The three parts of the feast should be blessed in the names of whichever powers or deities you feel to be appropriate. The bread/salt is offered around, either by one person offering it to all present or passed round from hand to hand. This is followed by the consecrated wine (you can use spring water or unfermented fruit juice if you wish, but most groups use real wine). Again, do not rush; make sure each person gets time to eat and drink, and when the last one has finished the bread and wine, and the empty goblet has been turned onto the platter, it is finished. You may also like to pass round a lighted lamp so that all can share the element Fire, and perhaps a scented flower, or carry round the incense burner with a few more grains of incense added. See what feels right for your group.

This is the culmination of the ritual, after which you will need to gently unwind, beginning with prayers to each of the four quarters, for peace, for plenty, and for healing, remembering especially anyone known to you. Lastly, pray for the companionship of all who tread the mystic path and who, though they may be unknown to you, are striving for the same sorts of things.

Reverse the carrying round of the elements, placing each on the altar; if it has been lodged at the edge of the circle, then walk round in the reverse direction yourselves, perhaps saying the self-blessing with its gesture as you do so, so that you gradually unwind your magical nature, coming firmly back to earth and this level of reality. Quietly disrobe, clear up, dispose of the dregs of wine and crumbs, and change out of your magical state.

Do not discuss the ritual with 'outsiders'. Shakespeare wrote: 'Peace, the spell's wound up. . . ', and he was right. You must allow the power to get on with the job, settle down and work in its own level of reality. Perhaps you noticed some strange shapes in the smoke of the incense; perhaps the candle flames seemed to flicker or sway in an odd fashion; perhaps one of you forgot a line, or moved in the wrong direction. Well, it is over. Write all the details into your magical diary, and then as far as possible, forget all about the matter. Like a seed, once planted, a magical act will not benefit from being dug up to see how it is getting on. Be patient, and in the next few days leave time to meditate on the objective and then you will receive information, hints or inspiration. You might also simply discover that whatever it was you performed the ritual for comes to pass.

Magical Festivals
As well as practical rituals there are many festivals that can be celebrated in a magical way. If the path to which you are drawn is that of witchcraft, you will find that any rites you come across or take part in with a coven will be

more religious in form. There are a series of traditional festivals that enact the year of nature, and in which the Goddess and God, portrayed sometimes by the High Priestess and High Priest of a group, act out their meeting, mating and the bringing forth of the Child of Promise at the Winter Solstice. The festival of Brigid, Bride or Candlemas, at the beginning of February is when the Goddess, who bore her son at Yuletide, returns as Goddess of Nature and is feted with snowdrops and other early spring flowers. Next comes the Spring Equinox when the sun enters Aries on about 21 March (check the exact dates and times of solar and lunar feasts in an ephemeris). At this time of equal day and night there is a celebration of the sown seed, the re-emergence of life in the spring flowers. Day and night are equal, so the God and Goddess should stand together, and this is their time of mating if the new Sun God is to be born at Yuletide.

At the end of April is May Eve, the wedding of the Goddess and God. The Goddess is magically changed into a white hind and the God, as the Hunter, seeks her in the woodland. After the chase they may dance and jump over a bonfire, the Beltane fire, named after the Sun God, Bel or Baal. There may be a wedding feast and houses are decked with Hawthorn blossoms, unlucky at any other time.

After May Day with its child May Queens enacting the bridal procession of the pagan Goddess, the Sun continues to climb to his zenith at midsummer and enters Cancer on or about 21 June. Here the God of Summer and of Winter fight for domination. At the beginning of August is Lammas or Loaf-mas, the time when the first corn was reaped and turned into bread. Here the God is the Spirit of the Corn and his sacrifice is enacted as told of in the song 'John Barleycorn'. He is cut down and laid into the arms of the Goddess, his widow and mother. The last sheaf of corn is saved and from it are made the Corn Dollies, or Kern Kings, representing Cernunnos, the antlered solar God as the spirit of nature. This is part wake and part celebration and both aspects ought to be shown in rituals at this time.

September brings the Autumnal Equinox on or about the 23rd, and the old feast now known as Michaelmas. St Michael who threw down, but did not kill the 'devil', is the name given to another solar God. High places and chapels built on mounds are often dedicated to St Michael or St George, who slew his dragon. Michael has taken over from Bran the Celtic solar God, represented by both the crow or raven and the Alder tree, whose wood bleeds red like blood yet lasts forever under water. This is a harvest festival in pagan circles, when fruits, nuts and garlands of late flowers are brought in to the circle to be offered to the God and Goddess.

Hallowe'en is the best known of the old feasts. Games of divination, looking in mirrors at midnight, bobbing for apples (the tree of knowledge and immortality) or eating them from strings enacts the battle for life in death. It is a time of ghosts and weird stories, but as a pagan rite it is the time when the dead and the living and the unborn children step outside the circle of time to meet, to talk and to exchange information. The door of the circle is left open and a place is laid with rich food and wine to be offered to the Goddess when she joins her worshippers, who are her children.

The last festival, at the time of Christmas, is Yuletide. It is in part the Winter Solstice on 21 December, part the feast of Mithras, a Persian Sun God who was born in a cave on about 25 December. The Goddess brings forth the infant Sun God and is offered candles, garlands of holly for the God and Ivy for the Lady. Mistletoe, the sacred Golden Bough of the Druids, whose white berries represent the seed of the Sun upon earth, is still not allowed in some churches. This strange 'All Heal' has not yet given up its secrets to herbalists, but it is often used by them. Yule (the word means 'wheel' in Saxon) is the turning point of the year, and the relighting of a great tree trunk from the nub of the last year's log symbolizes the continuity of light and warmth.

On 6 January the decorations are taken down and it is the end of the Twelve Days of Christmas. This, too, is a pagan festival, for it is the day when the Goddess presents her son, now twelve years old, to the people and when he is given his magical sword, shield (platter), arrows or lance (wand), and perhaps also a magical stone. He is paid homage to by all the participants and sent on his way, to shine over the world.

Not every coven follows this set of events but usually they have some form of ritual on each of the solar quarters and the cross quarters on or about these dates. Only traditional groups celebrate nine festivals, though most groups also have working rituals on the day of the full moon, or sometimes the nearest Saturday or convenient date. If you wish to study witchcraft you will see that there are plenty of chances to share feasting and ritual with friends and other witches, or you may prefer to work alone, as did the village witches in most parts of Britain. It is certain that each place had a healer, scryer and herbal expert, often one old lady or gentleman, or perhaps a family, though there is little evidence that the coven of thirteen witches existed in many places. Most of the evidence about witch groups was wrung from the accused under duress, although torture was never used in England, nor were witches here burned at the stake. Scotland used both torture and burning, but the information thus obtained is far closer to what the accusers thought witches ought to confess than what they actually did. It also assumes that the real wise folk were caught: most of them would have known psychically about any local witch hunts and kept out of the way. Many of the folk who were imprisoned or hanged were old men and women who had no one to stand up for them and probably lived by begging. Read any accounts of modern or ancient witchcraft with this in mind.

There are a small number of training lodges in Britain at present but they can only take in and teach a tiny percentage of all those who would wish for initiation into a regular, properly set up working lodge. Usually these require a period of study and work with other novices on different aspects of meditation, visualization, pathworking, symbolism, mythology and religion, psychology and the various traditions of magic. If you feel you would like to join such a group you will have to read the announcements in various occult journals very carefully to see if there are any vacancies or fresh training courses beginning. There are also postal courses.

Scientific Perspectives

The purpose of this book has been to encourage each individual to make the best possible use of all his or her innate skills, abilities and strengths, and by trying to grow into the light of knowledge, gain experiences that will help all mankind. You began by learning techniques to expand your understanding of yourself and the world you live in. You will be surprised how the simple-seeming exercises will have effects upon you, perhaps explaining long-held problems or doubts, opening new vistas of knowledge and experience, leading you to deeper understanding. If you are able to continue practising these basic arts you will develop magical abilities and perceptions far beyond what you might imagine. You will be able to relax in times of stress, your health will improve and your mind become clear and retentive. You will discover joy in living and the freedom brought about by being able to see many aspects of any situation and being able to exploit what is the best path.

Recent scientific experiments have demonstrated that the two halves of the human brain function in different ways. One half, the left, is concerned with logic (for instance, mathematical thinking) and it is most closely linked to the right side of the body. The right half of the brain is more perceptive, intuitive, aware of subtleties, and it controls the left side of the body. The exercises of the magician go a long way in bringing both halves of the brain into play at once. The use of imagination and creative visualization, which are the most powerful tools of modern occult work, together with the practical, physical skills of movement, making, designing and assembling talismans, brings all aspects of mentation into work. This helps to bring about a balance between the 'intellectual' type and the 'earthy, emotional' type of person, so that the perfect mage is competent in both modes of thinking.

Although it may seem a far cry from magic, the work of modern sub-atomic particle physicists is surprisingly close to some occult work. In Fritjof Capra's book *The Tao of Physics* he explains that the movements of the minute particles within the atoms are cosmic dances, such as are described in Hindu mythology. The gods dance and the world is created; we now know that the electrons, protons and neutrons match this dance, which conforms the bonds of continuity (which the magician manipulates) throughout the universe.

Many of the latest discoveries in science, rather than refuting magic as nonsense, seem to indicate that some of the ancient arts hold keys to processes within man and the universe that had not been fully understood before. In the field of parapsychology, experiments to project consciousness away from the physical body to view scenes and activities miles away follow the traditional ideas about 'astral travel', and these have been demonstrated in the laboratory. In order to help subjects achieve this they sit relaxed in a dimly lighted room perhaps lulled by white noise or soft music and often a kind of pathworking is given to help them get away from their immediate surroundings. Certainly experiments in hypnosis, altered states of consciousness and other varied forms of inner awareness and control very closely match the magical model, known in the temples of ancient Egypt and the Druids' groves. These altered states are thought to be valuable keys to understanding the processes in man of pain control, or recovery from illness, injury or cancer and the like. There are such vast areas of life and living that are still not understood. Yogis have demonstrated for hundreds of years that they can slow their heart beat, stop breathing for long periods, remain warm whilst sitting naked in the snow, and walk on red hot stones. It is true that these events occur, but as they are magical techniques they have not been readily available for study outside the secret temple or hidden school. Now we are seeing serious study being given to control of blood pressure through biofeedback, or the easing of migraine pain by altering the flow of blood from the head to the hand. Patients can even learn to slow their heart beat and relax without drugs.

Music

The effects of sound are being studied, as well as the changes to breathing and blood supply caused by rhythmic chanting, previously only known by the occult teachers. Music is a very powerful medium and it can be used to excellent effect in ritual. It can help if you are shy and do not like speaking or singing. You can devise entire rituals of music instead of words. The most familiar piece of ritual music is that of the 'Planets Suite' by Gustav Holst. Although astrologically the music does not quite fit, each 'planet' does have a very valuable influence on anyone using it for meditation or ritual. Much classical music can be used for effect or to space out the action of ritual. Prayers or incantations can be said to a musical background, giving power and timbre to your voice. Each session of meditation or pathworking can be accompanied by some appropriate sounds or soothing instrumental backing. Although classical music has something suitable for all moods and all stages of any ritual and can be selected to represent invocations of the elements and so on, there are many modern composers whose works are also fitting. Mike Oldfield's various synthesiser compositions can be ideal if you like that sort of music; and Steve Halpern, who writes music specially designed for meditation and mood softening, has a wide selection of tapes now available.

It is another vast field of research and experiment, and like all aspects of occult work, the more effort you put into it the better the results will be. If you have an important ritual pending it is an opportunity to make sure that all the equipment, regalia and background music are in complete harmony with your intentions. Again, do not rush into anything. As has been said all through this work , you are entering a huge field of study which has no clearly defined edges. You can practise ritual, divination, astrological interpretation, study the Qabalah or mythology for the rest of your life without coming to anything like limits of the subject.

Perhaps you will have had the opportunity to sample some of the most basic magical skills and are already looking forward to an age when occult matters have their true place beside what is usually called science and religion. Perhaps you have already been able to open some windows on your world, seen new horizons, gained new insights. Perhaps you have already begun to come to terms with who you are, and who you might become if you apply yourself to creating a better, clearer, stronger, more efficient self, aided always by the inner you. Any change is probably only a beginning. This may not seem so romantic and glamorous as you had thought magic might be; but magic is predominantly a practical art. There is a place for glamour and show, within the lodge — worshipping, calling aid from the higher powers, giving thanks and receiving blessings; and you may go in for the most elaborate regalia and the most costly settings you can devise. In the world, however, you will need discretion, capability and the skill to cope with *human* situations.

This is just a beginning. Its end may be many lives hence, when man is using his skills to know, to learn, to heal and to intuit on distant planets. We cannot see where man's destiny will lead him, any more than the medieval alchemists (whose psychological texts are only now being fully understood). But one thing is certain: the arts of magic are not those of a forgotten age, outgrown and fit only to be cast aside like an old coat. They are the skills of the mind, and that is a region on this well-charted planet that is scarcely known at all. With imagination, with creative ability and with common sense we can take magic from the hidden cupboards into all aspects of human experience. We may have not yet grown into Aquarian people, but we do have the keys to Aquarian Magic, as we have had them through all past ages. All we need now is the skill, the daring and the patience in which to use them.

CONCLUSION

If you have simply read through this book you might wonder how it could be called a book of magic; but if you have already tried some of the exercises, or have learned some of these ancient arts from another book, you will have been able to experience some of the fascination of the enthralling practices, the strange arts that suddenly begin to *work* — to produce results and unfold information previously hidden from you.

This is not the end, though, by any means. To become skilled in the magical arts may take many years, for there is such a vast field to cover. It is for this reason that it is suggested that you read a great deal more, continue with the basic exercises until they are second nature, and, if at all possible, find a friend or two who can share your work. Once you have mastered the first steps in magic it is up to you to choose a system, perhaps apply for membership of a group, or join a training course. You will need to read books on a broad spectrum of subjects — psychology, magic, comparative religion, the Qabalah, ancient history, mythology, poetry, ritual, witchcraft, country spells, as well as practical arts such as costume making, embroidery, woodcarving, painting, brewing of sacred wines and baking special cakes for your ceremonies. You will need to master the lists of correspondences, discover gums and scents that apply to all the planets and for any other form of magic. You may wish to study healing arts, grow herbs and study music and dance to enliven your rituals. As you go on, there is no limit to the situations into which your wider magical knowledge may lead you — life will be full of surprises, it will be healthy, joyful and enthralling, filled with wonder and child-like delight.

FURTHER READING

This is only a selected list of some of the more relevant books covering the material in this book.

Dolores Ashcroft-Nowicki, *Building an Occult Temple* (Pallas Aquariana)
_____ , *First Steps in Ritual* (Aquarian Press).
J.H. Brennan, *Reincarnation: Five Keys to Past Lives* (Aquarian Press).
Charles Bowness, *The Practice of Meditation* (Aquarian Press).
W.E. Butler, *Apprenticed to Magic* (Aquarian Press).
David Conway, *Magic: An Occult Primer* (Mayflower).
Dion Fortune, *The Mystical Qabalah, The Training and Work of an Initiate* (Aquarian Press).
Tom Graves, *Dowsing* (Turnstone Press).
Marian Green, *Magic in Principle and Practice* (Quest).
_____ , *The Paths of Magic* (Quest).
Brian Inglis, *Natural Medicine* (Fontana).
Gareth Knight, *A History of White Magic* (Aquarian Press).
_____ , *Occult Exercises and Practices* (Aquarian Press).

Israel Regardie, *Foundations of Practical Magic* (includes the
   essay 'The Art of True Healing') (Aquarian Press).
Doreen Valiente, *Witchcraft for Tomorrow* (Hale).
Colin Wilson, *Mysteries* (Mayflower).
⸻ , *The Occult* (Mayflower).

FURTHER INFORMATION

There are dozens of small magazines, local suppliers and book sellers, both in shops and by mail order, but because these change their address, close down, or merge with other similar businesses, it is not possible to give a comprehensive list. The most enduring of these dealers are listed below and *Prediction* magazine, published monthly and available from any newsagent, frequently advertises publications, training schools, suppliers of incenses and so on.

ATLANTIS BOOKSHOP, 49A Museum Street, London WC1 deals in most current books.

MARGARET BRUCE, High Rigg House, St John's Chapel, Bishop Auckland DL13 1QT supplies incenses, herbs, talismans, oils, etc. by post only, in UK.

PALLAS AQUARIANA, BM Opal, London WC1N 3XX supplies pure gums, incense burners, rare magical texts and publishes *Aquarian Arrow* on magic.

THE SERVANTS OF THE LIGHT ASSOCIATION, PO
   Box 215, St Helier, Jersey run a postal course of
   instruction based on the works of W.E. Butler and
   Gareth Knight, and publishes *Round Merlin's Table*
   quarterly.

SAROS, Hardwick Hall, Hardwick Square, Buxton,
   Derbyshire is a residential course centre, providing
   weekend and longer courses on self-awareness, Qabalah,
   magic, and healthy living.

DUSTY MILLER AND SON makes all the wands, rods,
   charms and symbols of the Old Religion from wood
   and natural objects. 14 Weston Road, Strood, Kent
   ME2 3EZ.

SORCERER'S APPRENTICE, 4/8 Burley Lodge Road,
   Leeds LS6 1QP. Rare herbs, oils, scents, incenses,
   temple requisites.

QUEST, BCM SCL QUEST, London, WC1 N 3XX, edited
   by Marian Green since 1970, is published each quarter
   and deals with all aspects of modern magic. There is
   also an Annual Conference in London each March and
   the *Quest* team runs two postal courses; one a Ritual
   Magic, and the other on Natural Magic/Witchcraft.
   Quest also arranges local meetings of the Green Circle,
   an open study group, with occasional weekend residential
   courses on magic, healing, etc.

AQUARIAN PRESS publishes new and classic books on
   magic, astrology, self-development, mysticism and
   esoteric thought. Full catalogue sent on request:
   Denington Estate, Wellingborough, Northamptonshire
   NN8 2RQ.

There are a number of Festivals each year all over Great
Britain concerned with health, psychic development,
self-awareness and meditation. Further information will
be found in the national press or in the relevant magazines.

INDEX